The Governance Core is a masterp

to seize the moral high ground, establish a unity of purpose, and pursue governing excellence. The book is insightful, engaging, and filled with real-world examples that illuminate important principles needed for effective governing. *The Governance Core* is a must-read for new or veteran school board members.

—**Vernon Billy,** CEO and Executive Director
California School Boards Association

Brilliant and utterly compelling! I have sat in boardrooms for 46 years governing education institutions, hospitals, and universities. It's as if Davis Campbell and Michael Fullan were looking over my shoulder! *The Governance Core* captures the essence of effective governance in complex times. This book challenges us to focus on and achieve a higher moral purpose. Campbell and Fullan move beyond what governance is and explore how great leaders should govern.

—**Bill Hogarth,** Consultant and Former Director of Education
York Region District School Board

Governance, school boards, and superintendents are on the front line of meeting the challenges facing education in the 21st century. *The Governance Core* by Davis Campbell and Michael Fullan captures not only the nature of the challenges but also the characteristics of highly successful school board trustees and superintendents working together. *The Governance Core* goes deeply into the heart of effective governance. Incorporate these ideas, and you will become much more effective as governance leaders—and your students, parents and educators will benefit immensely.

—**Frank Pugh,** Past President
National School Boards Association

A treasure of a book, chock-full of guidance from the strategic to the pragmatic. I will refer to *The Governance Core* regularly as our board and principal work together in the service of the scholars and families in our school community. Whether you're a district leader or a principal, on a district school board, charter board, or local school council, you will find insights and tools to deepen your understanding and improve your practice of effective governance. Our nation's children deserve no less.

—Susan Lucas, Co-Chair, Legacy Charter School, Chicago, IL

Davis Campbell and Michael Fullan do a masterful job of explaining how public school boards and superintendents working well together, with a shared moral imperative, can be a driving force for improvement in student learning as well as for society as a whole. This exquisite new book, *The Governance Core,* beautifully explains why this is true and how to achieve it.

—Leslie DeMersseman, Past President
California School Boards Association

Simultaneously visionary and pragmatic, *The Governance Core* provides a comprehensive, action-oriented blueprint for designing an effective governance system focused squarely on what matters: student learning. Davis Campbell and Michael Fullan demonstrate how the right approach to governance can make the critical difference in achieving learning for all students. This new book is a powerful, persuasive must-read not only for superintendents and school board members but also for all of us in nonprofits and public agencies who share a commitment to students' succeeding in school and beyond.

—Glen Harvey, Chief Executive Officer, WestEd

Good governance is a skill, a discipline, and a commitment. Davis Campbell and Michael Fullan reveal new understandings and important lessons about governing public school systems for healthier communities. They make the compelling case that effective governance in these uncertain times is an essential driver for a better democracy. A must-read for all new and veteran board members and superintendents.

—Tony Smith, Former State Superintendent of Education
Illinois State Board of Education

Davis Campbell and Michael Fullan have provided great insights on the governance core in this inspiring book. I recommend that trustees and superintendents read this book together—and act on the key messages.

—John Malloy, Director of Education
Toronto District School Board

The Governance Core

School Boards, Superintendents, and Schools Working Together

Davis Campbell
Michael Fullan

Forewords by Frank Pugh and John Malloy

A JOINT PUBLICATION

A SAGE Publishing Company

FOR INFORMATION:

Corwin

A SAGE Company

2455 Teller Road

Thousand Oaks, California 91320

(800) 233-9936

www.corwin.com

SAGE Publications Ltd.

1 Oliver's Yard

55 City Road

London EC1Y 1SP

United Kingdom

SAGE Publications India Pvt. Ltd.

B 1/I 1 Mohan Cooperative Industrial Area

Mathura Road, New Delhi 110 044

India

SAGE Publications Asia-Pacific Pte. Ltd.

18 Cross Street #10-10/11/12

China Square Central

Singapore 048423

Publisher: Arnis Burvikovs

Development Editor: Desirée A. Bartlett

Senior Editorial Assistant: Eliza B. Erickson

Production Editor: Melanie Birdsall

Copy Editor: Lynne Curry

Typesetter: Hurix Digital

Proofreader: Caryne Brown

Indexer: Molly Hall

Cover Designer: Scott Van Atta

Marketing Manager: Sharon Pendergast

Printed in the United States of America

Library of Congress Cataloging-in-Publication Data

Names: Campbell, Davis W., author. | Fullan, Michael, author.

Title: The governance core : school boards, superintendents, and schools working together / Davis Campbell and Michael Fullan.

Description: Thousand Oaks : Corwin, [2019] | Includes bibliographical references and index.

Identifiers: LCCN 2019000043 | ISBN 9781544344331 (pbk. : alk. paper)

Subjects: LCSH: School board-superintendent relationships—United States. | School management and organization—United States. | Educational leadership—United States.

Classification: LCC LB2831 .C26 2019 | DDC 371.2/011—dc23 LC record available at https://lccn.loc.gov/2019000043

This book is printed on acid-free paper.

21 22 23 10 9 8 7 6

Contents

Foreword

Frank Pugh

Past President,
National School Boards Association

Because of the privilege of serving as President of National School Boards Association in 2018–19, I have had the benefit of meeting and working with school board trustees and superintendents from every part of this great country. Education is changing. And I believe it's changing for the good. But with changes come incredible difficulty and challenges. Governance, school boards, and superintendents are on the front line of meeting those challenges. Some are doing a great job; others are struggling.

The Governance Core by Davis Campbell and Michael Fullan is the first book that captures not only the nature of the challenges but also the characteristics of highly successful school board trustees and superintendents working together. Campbell and Fullan don't lecture or preach, and they don't just give the traditional lists of dos and don'ts (although there are a few of those). *The Governance Core* goes much deeper into the heart of effective governance.

Perhaps most powerful is the emphasis on the characteristics of highly effective trustees. Effective trustees, to a person, operate with a governance mindset. They understand that governance is much more than just coming to meetings and voting. As a 28-year experienced local school district trustee, I found the four essential characteristics of the governance mindset outlined in the book—systems thinking, strategic focus, deep learning, and managing public manner—not only on target but reassuring that someone has finally put it all on paper. Campbell and Fullan's framework captures what many of us see in our colleagues who are having a powerful impact on the children in their districts.

I especially recommend the chapters on coherence, the moral imperative, and welcoming new school board members. It is important for new
trustees to hit the ground with all the tools they need to begin their governance journey. The book contains many practical suggestions for helping
make the transition for elected trustees, from campaigning to governing.
Having a well-thought-out plan for onboarding new trustees also helps veteran board members review and recommit to effective governance practices. The analysis and recommendations throughout the book will help
all trustees and superintendents examine their own roles, especially their
roles in relationships when they are working together for maximum effect.

I found the extensive discussion of a shared moral imperative driving a unity of purpose on the board an essential part of effective governance. Campbell and Fullan emphasize the importance of developing a
cohesive, unified board, with superintendent and board working closely
together. I particularly found the identification and discussion of the
challenges boards face in developing this coherence well developed and
authentic. Almost all boards at one time or another are faced with one or
more of these challenges. *The Governance Core* takes ten of these, one by
one, and provides succinct practical suggestions for resolving them.

What many of us with years on a school board understand is that
governing effectively requires structure and discipline. Campbell and
Fullan show how governance principles, norms, and protocols adopted by
the board can provide the necessary infrastructure to govern effectively.
They further discuss four governance tools—discussion meetings, governance handbooks, board self-evaluation, and board continuing governance
education—that supply the practical, hands-on assistance that every board
member needs.

This book is a must-read for every school board trustee, superintendent, and anyone seeking to understand how effective governance works.
Read this book individually and together. You will become much more
effective as governance leaders, and your students, parents, and educators
will benefit immensely.

Foreword

John Malloy

Director of Education,
Toronto District School Board

I t is amazing to me that something as crucial as effective governance is not written about more often. Many assumptions and perspectives exist about what effective governance is, but seldom do we see this important topic addressed with such candor and clarity. Davis Campbell and Michael Fullan have provided great insights for us to consider in this inspiring text on the governance core.

As a Director of Education (superintendent) at the Toronto District School Board (TDSB), working with 22 elected trustees and staff, students, and parents in 583 schools, I know firsthand how critical effective governance is as our board strives to fulfill the strategic commitments we have made. When I am working cohesively with the board, we can achieve so much. That said, this unity and cohesion would be fleeting if we were not intentional about how we work together—the governance core that is formulated by Campbell and Fullan does just that. The main message is that the focus of governance must be on system improvement. We need to make our schools places where our students can achieve great heights while also growing as healthy individuals. Our work as educators, supported by the board, needs to add value to every aspect of our children's school experience. We know that challenges sometimes exist in our schools and in our school systems, and inequities can also prevail. Part of adding value to the lives of each and every student in our school district means that courageous leadership is also required to name what isn't working, to remove obstacles and barriers, and to monitor the commitments that have been made. Campbell and Fullan have helped us think about how to be intentional in terms of effective governance so that at the end of the day our students thrive.

It is essential that superintendents working with their board understand how to support the board to be strategic and to focus on the entire system. In other words, the superintendent must see the work of the board as central to the success of the district. Similarly, it is equally critical for the board to have confidence in the expertise of the superintendent. Without this confidence, effective governance erodes. I especially appreciated that the authors' attention centers on the importance of the board being informed, focused, and engaged. I also appreciated reading how trust can be eroded particularly if a trustee might believe that the staff is not providing appropriate, complete, or accurate information for example. This perspective around information could lead to difficult dynamics at board meetings. Campbell and Fullan provide important considerations to avoid something like this happening.

I very much valued the emphasis on the moral imperative stated throughout this book that drives our joint work between the superintendent and the board. This moral imperative is always focused on students. It is also essential for our public to have confidence in the work that is happening in schools and on school boards. This confidence is enhanced when the board and superintendent are seen as modeling effective governance practices. Most important, this confidence is strengthened when schools and school boards are fulfilling their most important goal, which is to provide the very best learning environment for each and every student. The governance core discussed in this book will certainly help boards and superintendents fulfill this privileged goal of service to all of our students. I recommend that trustees and superintendents read this book together—and act on the key messages.

Introduction
Politics, Governance, and System Improvement

· ·

The most remarkable thing about our country is this: ordinary citizens control almost every major institution, public and private . . . Does this make sense? What it makes is a democracy. We, the people, govern ourselves.

—Henry N. Brickell and Regina H. Paul, *Time for Curriculum* (1988)

Today, with how much is at stake in the success of our nation's institutions, especially public schools, Brickell's observation doesn't go nearly far enough.

What if more than merely extolling the democratic principles underlying it, we considered how local education governance could, in every district, become an exemplar of highly *effective* decision making, leadership, and action? Effective, as in major expansion in the capacity of local entities to bring about significant measurable improvements in the learning and lives of all students under their watch and care.

We believe that most trustees want to make a difference in the lives of students and to improve the district and the system as a whole. Strangely, they get little help in defining and fulfilling this role. Paul Richman, former Executive Director of California's Parent Teacher Association, drew a similar conclusion when he made the following comments to us:

> At a time when taking a coherent, system-wide approach to serving all kids and improving schools is more important than ever, effective governance is perhaps the least understood and most underutilized component for success and sustainability. School board members, superintendents, and their local communities especially need to understand and focus on effective governance. (personal communication, August 2018)

UNITY OF PURPOSE: DRIVEN BY A SHARED MORAL IMPERATIVE

That is what this book is about. Our vision is of a governance system, school board, and superintendent working together as a cohesive, unified team with a common vision driven by a shared moral imperative. This is a dynamic, powerful role for school boards. It assumes that governance is a basic function of the organization, an integral part of the system, setting the direction of the district, assuring the achievement of strategic goals and the moral imperative, holding the district accountable, and providing leadership to the community. Most important, it is a governance system that fulfills its responsibility to all the children and the community it serves.

> Our vision is of a governance system, school board, and superintendent working together as a cohesive, unified team with a common vision driven by a shared moral imperative.

The question of the improvement of local education governance comes at a critical time for society. There are signs that the world is facing formidable, seemingly impossible obstacles with respect to both the physical and social climate. There is rapidly growing inequity between the rich and the poor in almost every country. Stress and anxiety among the young and old are becoming more marked and affecting younger and younger children. Trust in societies is worsening. Schooling is also becoming less and less engaging for the majority of students as they go up the grade levels. Education cannot be expected to solve everything, but it is increasingly clear that it is the one social institution that has the potential to make a major difference for humanity in a troubled world. On the positive side, we have new, powerful education ideas that have the potential to deepen learning for all students, especially those that are most disconnected from life and schooling (see Fullan, Quinn, & McEachen, 2018). More than ever we need effective core governance at the local level led by trustees and superintendents who not only work jointly with each other but also form powerful partnerships with their schools and communities.

We wrote this book because there is an urgent need for better and markedly more effective school districts. Trustees, superintendents, schools, and communities working together can generate this new social presence and power.

We will make the case that there has been little attention paid to the study and improvement of school district governance. The education research and reform communities have seriously neglected the potentially powerful role of governance in sustaining long-term improvement. People seem to think that "it is what it is." Too often given actions have become stereotypes, whether justified or not: individual trustees are often cast as the bad guys; boards as a whole are seen as part of a bureaucracy that is removed or unable to act responsively; and superintendents are cast as victims of meddling and micromanagement. In this way superintendents are absolved of building genuine working relationships with their boards, and we end up with variations on we-they relationships with best case scenarios from superintendents being "My board is great—they leave me alone to do my job."

In this book we take a different tack with local school boards and their trustees and superintendents. We go to the core, basic foundation of understanding local efficacy: the mindset of high-performing trustees and superintendents carrying out the critical function of governance.

We believe that school boards are vastly underutilized at precisely the time when they are most needed. We hold another fundamental premise that we will position in the course of this book: *the vast majority of school board members want to improve the public education system.* We are sure there are some bad apples or quirky self-interested individuals among the lot (as is the case with some superintendents). But the irony is that the neglect of the critical role of governance by the broader education community has made ineffectiveness a self-fulfilling prophecy for all too many districts. Many state school board associations have done a good job of providing training programs for trustees, but their capacity and ability to reach all school boards in any given state are limited. Our approach is to get at the heart of how to maximize unifying action of boards and superintendents together. That will benefit all students and all teachers (and in turn, parents and the public). Our point: we are in danger of squandering this potential because *we have almost totally neglected the vital function of school board governance within the larger system of education change.*

POLITICS, GOVERNANCE, AND SYSTEM IMPROVEMENT

The concepts of politics and governance are tricky because they have wide and varying definitions. Politics for example can have a positive, neutral, or negative meaning. Some definitions refer to politics as "the art of governing"; others refer to it as competing power struggles. Playing politics or office politics, or blatant attempts to get and keep power conceive of politics as negative. Overall, we are going to use it as meaning "holding and using power" which by itself does not mean that you can get things done just because you have power. Governance, on the other hand, concerns the day-to-day operation of government. So, bear with us and think of "holding and using power" as politics and "exercising authority on a daily basis" as governance. For the sake of clarity and to get to the solution— good *politics* and good *governance*—we need to contrast the two elements as they work out in real conditions. Let's step outside the United States to Quebec, Canada, and to Mexico, both of which have had recent elections.

In October 2018, the people of Quebec elected a new provincial government with a strong majority choosing "right of center," a party that had never held power—the Coalition Avenir Quebec (CAQ, "coalition for the future of Quebec"). Uncharacteristically, as the party's new elected leader, Francois Legault appears to have chosen governance along with politics when he first welcomed his new members of parliament:

Politics: Holding and using power

Governance: Exercising authority on a daily basis

> Our team must now create a government for Quebecers not a CAQ
> government. We will form a government for all Quebecers . . . We
> must also represent people who did not vote for the party, to put
> aside partisan considerations and act with the higher interest of
> Quebec in mind. (Authier, 2018)

Maybe this is good politics, but for us it also represents potential good governance (which remains to be seen in practice).

A few days later, the *New York Times* published an article about Mexico's president-elect Lopez Obrador titled *Faced With Reality of Job, Mexico's Next President Scales Back Promises* (Malkin, 2018). Lopez Obrador had been elected in July 2018 on a strong left-wing agenda of "battling corruption, soaring violence, and tackling entrenched inequality." He now faces (in our terms) the reality of governance. As one observer commented, "he is seeing Mexico with different eyes for the first time" (Malkin, 2018). Tackling Mexico's deep-rooted problems requires more than power and goodwill. In short, exercising power will not be sufficient; success will also require building a system of good governance in a country with long-standing weak infrastructure.

Fortunately for us, we are not trying to solve Quebec's or Mexico's problems, but the situation for local education governance is similar in kind. For the sake of argument and with slight exaggeration, we compare politics and governance in their negative and positive forms.

Politics Without Good Governance

- Peaks before, during, and just after elections
- Caters to special interest groups
- Often superficial: bumper-sticker style
- Can be sincere but weak on implementation
- Harmful when lacking good governance
- Limited lasting benefit

Politics With Good Governance

- Politics dominate during election
- Builds capacity relative to the core agenda

- Recognizes that government is for all of the people

- Long-term as well as short-term perspective

- Implementation versus adoption mindset

Our main goal in this book is to spell out what good governance consists of at the local district level so that well-intended politics can combine with the governance core to produce education results never before seen. We have one other major point that takes us back to the quote from Brickell and Paul at the beginning of this chapter. We need to update the meaning of "what makes for good democracy" in education. For us it means combining politics and good governance to achieve *system improvement* at both the local and state levels and in their interactive relationship. This is the essence of our book: *Good politics plus good governance wrapped in a systems perspective is the future of public education* (see Figure 0.1).

We are unabashedly forward about our solution: there needs to be a fundamental change in the culture and mindset of superintendents and board members in terms of how they see their roles and role relationships. Moreover, we predict that existing and future incumbents of these roles will embrace the new situations that we outline in this book once they experience and understand how they could operate differently in practice.

Figure 0.1 The Future of Education

Within this new mindset, we integrate Fullan and Quinn's (2016) parallel work in *Coherence: The Right Drivers in Action*. The coherence framework has become enormously popular among school districts seeking greater focus in their work. Yet the concept of "coherence" had barely found its way into governance discussions (two exceptions are the excellent work of the California School Boards Association and the Iowa School Boards Association), but even these examples did not go deeply into coherence in school board governance.

HOW THIS BOOK IS STRUCTURED

Part I contains four chapters that form the foundation of what we call *Mindsets for Efficacy,* which lies at the heart of the shift in culture we advocate. The chapters in turn examine the following: (1) the "Moral Imperative and the Governance Core"; (2) the "Trustee Governance Mindset"; (3) the "Superintendent Governance Mindset"; and (4)" Welcoming New Trustees."

In Part II, *Governing for Efficacy,* we take up the challenge of integrating coherence and governance in four chapters: (5) "Governing With Coherence"; (6) "Governance Culture"; (7) "The Governance Job"; and (8) "Governance Tools."

Part III takes the perspective of *The Challenges Ahead* with the concluding chapter, "Rising to the Occasion."

Together the chapters map out a new, more powerful system that we call the Governance Core.

Finally, in this introduction we want to frame the directional solution by returning to one of Fullan's fundamental concepts, *right and wrong policy drivers.*

SHIFT TO POSITIVE DRIVERS

As Fullan (2011) states, a driver is a policy intended to make a positive difference in practice. A wrong driver is a policy that turns out not to make a difference and, in some cases, actually backfires. Fullan identified four "wrong drivers" (punitive accountability, individualism, technology, and ad hoc policies). The corresponding right drivers were capacity building, collaboration, pedagogy, and systemness (when most people realize and act with the system in mind).

Systems thinking represents a situation where people are concerned with their own role expectations, but also see themselves as part of a bigger picture. They realize that their responsibilities extend to contributing to the bigger entity and to learning from others. The result is greater satisfaction for individuals and greater efficacy for the system itself.

Sorting out right and wrong drivers is at the heart of effective governance. Our solution is to frame the agenda around the right drivers for local governance. Systems thinking mainly involves the capacity to see one's role in the larger perspective of what other factors and relationships might be determining actions and outcomes. Such thinking is based on the orientation: how do I carry out my own role in a way that I contribute to and benefit from the larger system locally and beyond? The positive and negative drivers described in Figure 0.2 provide content to this shift we will pursue in subsequent chapters.

The eight so-called negative drivers are by and large what we have now. They narrow the agenda, present endemic frustrations, and unwittingly hamper the work and impact of local governance. A shift to the positive drivers represents a change in culture, mindset, and behavior. That means it will not be easy. We devote the rest of this book to detailing what this change in mindset looks like and how to achieve more of it. Once

Figure 0.2 **Governance Drivers**

Negative Drivers	Positive Drivers
1. Focus on school boards	1. Focus on governance
2. Focusing on board behavior	2. Focusing on governance mindset
3. Board presentations (audience)	3. Engaging the board (owner)
4. Counting votes	4. Counting understanding
5. Tactical (operations) driven agenda	5. Strategic (goals) driven agenda
6. Damage control perspective	6. Proactive, forward-thinking culture
7. Care and feeding of the board	7. Supporting the governance functions of the board
8. Board-superintendent relations	8. Board-superintendent cohesion

board members and superintendents see and experience what it entails, it will become more attractive. After their constituents (teachers, students, parents), and their "bosses" (the electorate, and policymakers, elected or otherwise) also experience the success of the positive drivers, they will become both more excited about and committed to their own roles. Put differently, it is in the best interest of school board members and superintendents to become more effective in improving the lot and learning of all of those whom they are expected to lead. We do know that quality change stands or falls at the local level. If we want systems to change, as we surely do, we'd better enlist the power of local governance with its schools and communities.

Fullan's work on examining wrong and right policy drivers led to the development of what would constitute a set of "right drivers for action." The result was a framework based on the integrating concept of *Coherence* (Fullan & Quinn, 2016).

Coherence is not alignment. Alignment occurs when the main pieces are aligned, such as goals, finances, professional development, assessment, and so on. By contrast, coherence is the *subjective* side of alignment. In a nutshell, alignment is rational while coherence is emotional. To reach a "shared depth of understanding" people must interact on a continuous basis sorting out their differences and coming to a common understanding that guides and reflects action. It is this emotional commitment that leads to success.

Coherence: The shared depth of understanding about the nature of the work

Governance mindset: The core understanding of the basic principles of governance: systems thinking, strategic focus, deep learning, and managing manner

We examine the role of school boards by turning to their most important and basic function, governance, while showing how the concepts *governance mindset and coherence* raise the clarity, status, and efficacy of the roles of trustees and superintendents. Governance mindset refers to the shared attitudes and beliefs that school boards and superintendents must develop and possess related to the action and manner of governing.

CONCLUDING COMMENTS

We trust that the reader is sensing where we are heading. In order to gain a shared understanding, trustees and superintendents must engage in the give-and-take of ideas. In short, they must *interact with purpose.* There are two fundamental characteristics at stake for effective governing. The first is that school board members and superintendents must continually develop a governance mindset individually and together to become a unifying force for fulfilling the moral imperative of raising the bar and closing the gap for all students.

The second characteristic concerns the *content* of the governance mindset that, as we will see in subsequent chapters, consists of the moral imperative, systems thinking, strategic focus, deep learning, and manner. In this way, trustees and superintendents learn together to appreciate the big picture and the details that make the board effective or not. In the end, those with a governance mindset accomplish more—much more—for their local community and the larger system they serve.

Part I

....

Mindsets for Efficacy

1

Moral Imperative and the Governance Core

• •

Governance of local school districts by citizen boards is a basic tenet of American democracy. Given the increasing presence of conflict and the corresponding stress and tension in the public school system around the country, there has never been a time when highly effective governance is more needed. The delegation of responsibility for education to the state and subsequently to the local school districts as agents of the state, places local school boards as critical linchpins in the system. How well boards carry out their governance responsibilities in many ways determines the quality of the education for the children they serve.

While effective local governance was the original intent in establishing school boards, the system of local governance has evolved without much research and development of what might be the most effective forms of school boards and superintendents working together to maximize individual student learning. We maintain that the study of and development of ever better forms of effective local governance has been education's neglected child.

Democratic systems have changed dramatically over the past 200 years, all the more so in the past twenty years as expectations have risen, only to be increasingly thwarted. The digital world has ironically dramatically increased access to information while presenting greater confusion about what might be true or not. The role of education itself has become incredibly more complex: tackling growing inequity with many factors outside the control of school boards is ever more daunting; students are more diverse and different in so many ways; jobs and the economy are almost completely unpredictable; the world itself feels more mysterious and dangerous; anxiety and stress are on the rise for young and old alike. Almost everyone feels that he or she should have a say in the matter. Intuitively, it seems that quality education for all would be one of the very few positive pathways forward. All of this and more make the matter of governance remarkably complicated. Yet we would venture to say that very few, even those in decision-making positions, stop and think about "What is governance anyway?" In short, governance is crucial and neglected—so let's start with this elusive concept.

THE NATURE OF GOVERNANCE

We have already made the point that there is a big difference between politics and governance. Of course, there is always politics, but at certain times—such as before, during, and just after elections—blatant politics can distort the governance core we focus on in this book. At those times politics can lose perspective as it becomes preoccupied with single hot-button issues that are inevitably superficial or otherwise incomplete. Most effective solutions must consider diverse views and get beneath surface issues to take up the combination of factors essential for solving problems. In this sense we can see the governance core discussed in this book as a corrective factor for narrow agendas. We do recommend "focus," but also show across the chapters how the governance relationships between trustees and superintendents must develop mutual coherence over time if progress is to be achieved. Our advice then is "Yes, keep focused on your key priorities, but (a) take into account diverse views relative to implementing such matters, and (b) be open to other priorities that might be held by others, or might arise from the environment (but don't fall prey to "initiativitis" (a continuous stream of ad hoc new priorities and programs); nobody said the job was easy!)"

As an organizational function, governance is often misunderstood and underappreciated. Defining governance isn't easy because it is a lot of different things. Governance derives from the Greek word, *kubernésis,* "to steer a ship." Donald McAdams adds, "Simply put, governance is steering; management is rowing" (McAdams, 2005, p. 9). What is generally understood is the commonly held notion that school boards deal with policy and staff with administration. Unfortunately, it's not that simple. Governance is much more than just adopting policies. One of the unique aspects of local government in the United States is that unlike the federal and state government, the legislative, administrative and judicial functions are centralized under one governing authority, the elected or appointed school board. This has a major impact on the role of governance in the school district. Because the school board appoints the chief executive (the superintendent), an oversight and stewardship responsibility is created for the board in addition to the legislative (policy) function. While the notion that governing boards adopt policies is widely accepted, the responsibility of providing some level of school district oversight is not: at least not until something goes wrong.

Governance is the process where the direction of the organization is set, the structure is established, and accountability both fiscal and programmatic is assured. Governance is the connection between communities and professionals, between policy and application, between strategy and tactics. Generally, governance is about defining the "what" of the organization, and administration is focused on the "how" policy gets implemented. If the discussion is focused on long-term outcomes, it tends to be strategic; if it is about short-term objectives or incremental steps, it tends to be tactical or administrative.

Most research on governance to date has focused solely on relatively narrow board roles, rather than our approach, which focuses on how boards govern. Under a broad and rarely defined concept of "policy," the traditional definition of board responsibilities seems designed to inhibit or constrain the board's scope of leadership. But governance is not just passing policies; it is what boards and superintendents do together *and* how they do it.

> Governance is not just passing policies; it is what boards and superintendents do together *and* how they do it.

Governance is not just passing policies; it is what boards and superintendents do together *and* how they do it.

A FUNDAMENTAL CHOICE

A major decision for trustees on any board is how as a group they choose to govern. Governance is one of the few areas where participants have the option to choose how they will act without the overt pressure of external variables. No one forces a trustee or board to govern well or poorly. The choice is entirely theirs. Will they be a collection of individuals, coming together for meetings, each person with his or her own agenda, own vision, and seeing his or her main function as voting on unrelated issues with little if any coherence or consistency? There are those who argue that all trustees need to do is attend their board meetings and vote. Counting votes on the board becomes the most important skill. There are also those who claim that boards should be totally independent of the agencies they govern—that their fiduciary and oversight responsibilities require they maintain distance from the staff and the programs the agency administers. Or, as we argue in this book, will the board choose to create a cohesive, unified team working together to create a common vision driven by a shared moral imperative? This is a dynamic, powerful role for the board. It assumes that governance is a basic function of the organization, an integral part of the system, setting the direction of the district, assuring the achievement of strategic goals and the moral imperative, holding the district accountable and providing leadership to the community.

This is the critical fork in the road that all boards must face (see Figure 1.1). Their decision will, in large part, determine whether the board will lead the school district or will be sitting on the sidelines or, worse,

Figure 1.1 **A Fork in the Road**

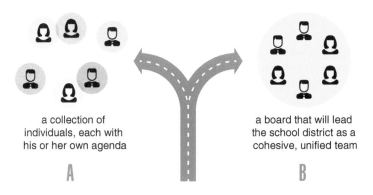

a collection of
individuals, each with
his or her own agenda

A

a board that will lead
the school district as a
cohesive, unified team

B

become a negative, incoherent force. Will the board own the programs they mandate or will they be observers? As observers, the board cannot be a part of the system-wide coherence making that is so fundamental to high-performing districts. As owners, the board should be the ultimate coherence maker. More important, the board can be the link that ensures long-term sustainability of successful programs that provide high-quality education for all students in the district.

There are currently 13,809 school boards with roughly 90,000 trustees governing school districts in every state in the United States. This book is a road map to high-quality, effective governance for school district trustees and superintendents in these districts. It is based on five major themes.

FIVE MAJOR THEMES OF GOOD GOVERNANCE

1. Making a commitment to *good governance*

2. A *shared moral imperative* that drives the work of the school board, the superintendent, and the strategic direction of the district

3. Highly effective trustees and superintendents who have a *governance mindset* to govern effectively

4. Effective school boards as coherence makers who govern with a *unity of purpose*

5. Leadership from the middle: System responsibilities

Make a Commitment to Good Governance

Effective school board governance makes a difference—a huge difference in the long-term success of quality education programs. The board and superintendent together can be an essential force for equity, excellence, and achievement. Donald R. McAdams, former trustee and president of the Houston Independent School district, is an expert on urban education governance. He writes in his book *What School Boards Can Do, Reform Governance for Urban Schools*,

> Only boards, because of the democratic power they derive from the people, because of their close links with the people, and because of their stability, can provide the leadership required to redesign and sustain over decades school districts that provide equity and the results for all children. That most have chosen not to do so is not an argument for stripping them of their power. Rather it is an argument for showing them how to exercise their power. (McAdams, 2005, p. 11)

What McAdams recognizes is that despite the difficulties and frequent controversies about school board governance, it is a fundamental part of the American educational experience. But much more important, effective board governance, when it works well, not only makes a significant contribution to the quality of education programs but also creates a long-term commitment to quality and continuous improvement. The key word is *effective*. This book is about putting in place a high-quality, effective governance system, the Governance Core, that will not only support high-quality instructional programs but will also create the stable, sustainable environment necessary for continued growth and improvement.

Commit to a Shared Moral Imperative

A shared moral imperative—a relentless commitment to the learning of all students, no exceptions—must drive the work of the board and its individual and collective action. We say that if there is not a clear moral imperative; if there is not a specific means of implementing it in practice;

and if there are not measurable outcomes that mark progress and attainment; and in the context of this book, if the board and the superintendent cannot articulate the state of play about the moral imperative as a system in action, then *it does not exist in reality.*

For many years, "vision" was seen to be the way forward. But over time vision has lost its cachet and become routine—time and again we see yet another vision statement and set of lofty goals about putting children first. As it turns out, "vision statements," as statements of intent, without being grounded in intensity of action, have poor track records. Every district has a vision statement on paper, but few of them get realized in practice. By contrast, our Governance Core Model is based on the depth of the moral imperative. The moral imperative *is* about all children learning. It consists of strategies to ensure that the learning occurs. It involves rapport between the trustees and the superintendent. It consists of strong focused relationships between the board and staff. It sorts out what is working and not in specific terms. It zeroes in on indicators of progress. It combines excellence and equity. At its heart, the Governance Core is a force for raising the bar and closing the gap of learning for all students in the district, not just as an aspiration, but as a reality. Beliefs are not strategies. In short, the moral imperative embodies an emotional and empirical commitment that *all children can and will learn.*

When trustees, superintendent, staff, faculty, and parents all operate with the same broad understanding of the moral imperative, the district can accomplish amazing learning—year after year. The moral imperative, deep focus, constructive monitoring, and corresponding action are an unstoppable combination. When this shared moral imperative is lacking, it is difficult to see how a long-term, stable governance system is possible, much less perform in an effective manner.

The moral purpose is geared to real, concrete educational goals for children. It is not so much a philosophical belief as it is a commitment to shared fundamental actions, such as the following:

- All children will achieve; we will not allow an achievement gap in our district.

- All children will have quality teachers.

- All children will be in a safe, healthy learning environment.

Governance Mindset

Governance mindset is a system phenomenon. The single most powerful governance force is the governance mindset displayed by the most successful, high-performing board trustees and superintendents. Governance mindset requires a fundamental understanding of all elements of the organization. Governance is about systems, not pieces.

> The single most powerful governance force is the governance mindset displayed by the most successful, high-performing board trustees and superintendents.

Thus, governance is a strategic, not an administrative, function. It is virtually impossible to effectively govern complex organizations such as school districts without the key policymakers and chief executive officers operating with a common mindset. At the outset, it is important for trustees to understand that governance, as an organizational function, is fundamentally different from administration and curriculum/instruction. Both curriculum/instruction and administration are functions carried out by administrators and teachers.

On the other hand, governance is a policy, strategic-based function. This is a crucial point because of the potential role confusion for board members if they do not understand this fundamental difference. Governance is a well-defined organizational function that requires specific skills different from administration and curriculum/instruction. Board members are elected to govern, not manage or teach. And to complicate matters even more, boards govern—not individual trustees.

We know of course that professionals in curriculum/instruction have an instructional/pedagogical mindset. In order to become an administrator, individuals go through extensive training and certification and develop an administrative mindset. So, doesn't it make sense that the governance function should also require a specialized mindset: one that is geared to the roles and responsibilities unique to governance?

Agree on a Unity of Purpose

Effective, powerful governance occurs when the board is operating in a unified, cohesive manner with a unity of purpose driven by the moral imperative. In governance, a unique dynamic transitional flow is created when a moral imperative is reached and transitions to a unity of purpose on the board. One of the best definitions of unity of purpose can be found in Long Beach Unified School District, the third largest school district in California, a complex, urban school district with a high-performing governance system.

> Unity of purpose is a common focus, super-ordinate goals and the core values and beliefs governance team members share in common about children, the district and public education. Unity of Purpose helps them transcend their differences to fulfill a greater purpose. (Long Beach Unified School District, 2003, *Governance Handbook)*

The starting place for developing a unity of purpose is around a central moral imperative from which programs and policies for the district flow. If there is disagreement among the board around this central point, then developing a unity of purpose on the board is almost impossible. Without a unity of purpose, then finding common ground around the basic work of the board becomes equally difficult. Finally, we have stressed that unity of purpose is not just about "words." If it is not rooted in action, it probably does not exist in any real sense.

Leadership From the Middle: System Responsibilities

Local school districts of course operate in the context of system policies and responsibilities. In our work on system change, we, and others like our colleague, Andy Hargreaves, have developed the concept of "Leading from the Middle" (LftM), (Hargreaves & Shirley 2018; Fullan & Quinn, 2016). You can't get system coherence from the top (too complex), and bottom-up change is too piecemeal. Where is the glue? We have found that one of the major sources of coherence is the middle of a state education system: school districts and other intermediate agencies working together. LftM has three main components: interpreting state policy, working laterally with other districts and regional entities to strengthen the middle, and what we call "liberating those below."

It works like this: with respect to the first element, school districts should be "proactive consumers" of state policy in relation to local priorities. There is an element of legal responsibility regarding finances and common goals, but, with respect to the latter, districts will need to interpret how local and state goals can best interface. The way we think of this is for districts to be proactive consumers of state policy vis-à-vis local priorities. Second, districts (school boards, superintendents, and schools) can join lateral networks and learn from each other. Such peer learning, as it does within schools when teachers collaborate, strengthens districts. Third, liberating downward, especially enabling groups to work together at other levels, further strengthens the overall system.

By being active, what we would call "system players," school boards, and superintendents become a valuable source of implementing as well as critiquing state policy. This is the essence of strategic governance. It is essential that school boards and superintendents not be simply receptacles receiving mandates from the state, but, rather, serious and powerful partners in the state policy process. As systems thinkers, trustees must not just think strategically as they lead their local districts but must look up and join with colleagues and superintendents to influence the policies that have such a major impact on their programs.

This role is crucial in all systems and is especially evident in California, where we work a great deal. With a policy of greater local control, less intrusive accountability, monitoring of progress through influence, and supportive capacity building, it is critical that school boards understand the complex interface of requirements and resources. And because they are a system in development, it is essential that districts become active players in the vertical and lateral interfaces that abound. In our view this is a good outcome. Instead of being on the receiving end of state policy, they can become better partners with their peers and other agencies regionally and at the state level. School boards with solid core governance capacity are in the best position to play this role as they get better results locally and contribute to the success of the overall system.

Striving for Common Ground

Sometimes individual trustees, for whatever reason, find it difficult to find common ground with fellow trustees on the board. When this occurs, it can jeopardize the ability of the board to develop a unified, cohesive governance team. If this happens, it is extremely important for the board not to give up but to take the time to try and work together, even in the face of deep differences and difficulties, to forge professional, respectful relationships. Effective governance requires that adults, on behalf of the children they serve, find avenues of agreement, so that they can govern the district in an effective manner. The responsibility of education governance is so profound that there is no acceptable alternative. The guidelines we recommend throughout this book should help ensure consistent good governance.

We acknowledge that now and then a situation arises where nothing seems to help. Our main recommendation is don't jump to this conclusion prematurely or before exploring other avenues. Addressing this challenge requires patience and the ability to continually re-focus the board's time on the work at hand, which is governing. There is no such a thing as a fix, but rather an approach that seeks to strengthen the relationships and culture over time. The following guidelines are important at all times for those serving on the board, but especially useful when there is friction with an individual trustee.

Guidelines for Serving on the Board (especially during times of friction)

1. Reserve judgment. Trustees with a governance mindset understand that making assumptions or holding on to preconceived views of other trustees, particularly individuals with divergent philosophical and ideological points of view, can seriously undermine the ability to communicate.

2. Listen empathetically. Oftentimes the manner or behavior of a person (especially one who has not yet adopted a governance mindset) distracts us from the substance of what they are saying. Remember to step back and be analytical so you can cut through issues of manner and behavior to understand the core message being given. Even the most aggressive trustee representing a minority view or opinion has important wisdom or perspective to offer. Be open to learning what the person is communicating.

3. Stay focused on content, not behavior or style. Ignore rhetoric. Do not allow issue differences to become weapons in personal disputes on the board. Remain committed to deep learning and to

understanding in depth the core issues of a moral imperative. It is okay to have many styles on a board, but there can be only one moral imperative.

4. Always be true to the norms of the board. It is at times of stress and difficulty that norms and protocols are most important. Treat every trustee with respect and demonstrate the core values of the board.

5. Do not take differences personally. Stay grounded as a systems thinker with a strategic focus. Remember the only behavior a person can control is his or her own. This can be admittedly challenging at times—we are all human—but the governance mindset requires it.

6. If all else fails after many attempts to accommodate the views or behaviors of a given trustee, it is important for the board to move forward in fulfilling its governance responsibilities. Irreconcilable differences or behaviors that repeatedly violate the agreed upon norms cannot be allowed to keep the board majority from doing its job. Nor can the board allow itself to become consumed by the situation at the expense of carrying out its critical responsibilities. If the board has been fair in trying to resolve the differences over time, the difficult board member will receive little support from peers. In most cases, however, issues will be resolved by following steps 1 to 5.

Reducing Friction With Good Governance

An incumbent, who was vice president of his board, was running for re-election. The board had a three-two split with the vice president one of the board majority. The incumbent was defeated in his election. The individual who won was perceived to be sympathetic to the point of view of the board members in the minority. The remaining two trustees of the previous majority were understandably upset and very antagonistic to the new trustee. It had all the elements of a potential highly charged dysfunctional governance dynamic.

However, the new trustee took the lead to establish a new culture. He treated all members of the board with respect and refused to be drawn into personal drama. He reached out to the two dissident board members to find common ground ignoring past disputes. It took time. But because the new trustee was resolute in his approach to governance, over time agreements became more common than disagreements. The board, despite differences, was working well together and with the superintendent. At the end of the new trustee's tenure on the board, one of the leaders of the dissident block made a motion of commendation praising the new trustee.

In short, personal disputes may not always be resolved readily, but following our guidelines above and those throughout this book will result in more productive outcomes in the vast majority of cases.

THE GOVERNANCE CORE

Let's return to the key theme and organizer of this book. One of the characteristics of school district governance is that in most cases it functions without an agreed upon, well-established theoretical structure. In many districts, governance is defined by what the board does when it meets, with little or any framework within which to work. Many school boards make up their modus operandi as they go. The basic functions are identified and understood: hiring the superintendent, approving policies, voting, all mostly driven by the board agenda; but there usually is limited definition of how best to carry out the full set of the board's responsibilities.

Our book is based upon the assumption that governance cannot be left to chance. Highly effective governance requires a well-defined infrastructure that provides definition, guidance, and direction.

> Highly effective governance requires a well-defined governance infrastructure that provides definition, guidance, and direction.

For a number of years, renowned Harvard professor Richard Elmore has focused on the importance of the instructional core in curriculum and instruction. The instructional core is about the relationship and interaction between the student, the teacher, and the content. The governance core presented here is based on the same principle of interdependence and symbiotic relationships. To be effective, trustees and superintendents must develop a governance mindset, a shared moral imperative, and unity of purpose utilizing sound principles and practices—the keys to effective governance.

We have organized the Governance Core into five main components (see Figure 1.2): Governance Mindset (Chapters 2, 3, and 4), Coherence (Chapter 5), Culture (Chapter 6), Jobs (Chapter 7), and Tools (Chapter 8).

The Governance Core represents an integrated, systemic approach to effective governance. It is dynamic, grounded in transforming a moral imperative to measurable, high-quality outcomes. As applied to education, these outcomes will substantially improve the life of children the system serves. This system is based upon a firm belief that successful organizations require a high level of coherence shared by boards of trustees,

Figure 1.2 **The Governance Core**

superintendents, staff, principals, teachers, and, yes, parents. All must share understanding of the nature of the work of the system. Once a moral imperative is shared, all aspects of the organization can be harnessed to deliver outstanding results. Boards can govern strategically, becoming deep learning organizations unto themselves.

CONCLUDING COMMENTS

In this book we take the position that trustees and superintendents must examine more comprehensively their core governance responsibilities. Investing time in establishing the governance core will yield multiple benefits. We believe that at the end of the day trustees and superintendents will find their work together to be much more satisfying and impactful. In short, we will all benefit!

2

Trustee
Governance Mindset

· ·

Just going through the motions of the form is not Tai Chi. It is excellent exercise, but it is not Tai Chi.

—Dr. Paul Lam, Master Tai Chi Instructor
(November 2011, Walnut Creek, CA)

After working with hundreds if not thousands of elected officials, we discovered that a common characteristic emerged that was present in all of the most effective trustees. These trustees, some who were leaders of the board and some not, demonstrated an intrinsic almost intuitive understanding about what it took to be effective as a trustee. They understood that in order to be effective, to do the job of governing, *all* members of the board had to be effective, not just a few. All trustees have to be leaders working together toward the same goals.

This understanding is what we are calling a *governance mindset*. The development of a governance mindset in our view is the most important characteristic of effective trustees. It is knowing how to think about governance, either intuitive or learned or both, and always, like a computer program running in the background, applying that knowledge and understanding (some would say wisdom) in real-time board work.

Having a governance mindset is understanding the role and responsibilities of the governing board and how individual trustee leadership can enhance the positive, value-added impact of the governance process. It is about understanding the difference between the function of governance and administration and curriculum and instruction. But more important, it's about understanding the ambiguity of the gray area that exists between the two and knowing when and how to navigate as a trustee. A particularly insightful trustee commented that having a governance mindset means becoming aware outside your own personal state of awareness. It has been referred to as "an attitude not an agenda."

This chapter will cover the four components of a governance mindset: systems thinking, strategic focus, deep learning, and manner. Developing this mindset first often requires a shift in thinking: We call this shift moving from I to We.

Part of the unique challenge facing trustees is that much of the work presents very difficult contradictions. The key to managing these challenges is developing a keen sense of internal balance. For example, having a governance mindset means establishing an internal balance between conflicting and very different values, concepts, intellectual positions, and core beliefs of the board. Developing a governance mindset is a difficult transition for many trustees.

Once trustees achieve this sense of governance mindfulness they tend to demonstrate a deeper understanding of the work of the board. They learn what works and what doesn't; they intuitively understand that the board must work together as a governance team rather than a group of individuals meeting in the same room moving in many directions with different agendas. They recognize the importance of coherence both within the board and within the district.

Because the concept of a governance mindset is a way of thinking, it can be useful to think about other examples where mindset plays an important role. For example, it is not uncommon to hear attorneys say they really learned about the details of law when they went into practice. What they learned in law school was how to think like a lawyer. And, in fact, despite all the differences in the practice of law, the common denominator is that effective lawyers think about issues from a similar legal perspective. The practice of law has a certain agreed-upon ethos to which lawyers adhere regardless of which side is being represented. Lawyers think like lawyers. Likewise, effective trustees think like trustees with a governance mindset.

Anyone who is conscientiously living a healthy life knows that the key lies in being mindful about choices. It means watching your diet, your weight, exercise, having spiritual connections, reducing tension, and making family a priority. Likewise, having a governance mindset means being aware and understanding the impact of every variable that affects the health of your organization.

Having a Governance Mindset Means

- Always keeping the board's focus on the children

- Watching the budget

- Keeping focused on the long-term goals of the organization

- Building and maintaining a strong governance infrastructure

- Supporting the staff and creating a positive organizational culture

- Holding the organization accountable to the community it serves

- Keeping the constituents of the organization informed and up to date on the work of the organization

In operation, a governance mindset is much more than just understanding. It is about having an internal moral compass geared to a well-defined moral purpose A high-performing trustee knows that excellence in governance requires purposeful action. This book is about that purposeful action. Those involved in achieving greatness in sports know that excellence in achieving success in any individual action is the result of extensive preparation (practice) and attention to the details of all the pieces leading up to that action. Any team sport—and being on a board is a team sport—requires everyone on the team to perform at the highest levels and understand his or her part in the process and how that contributes to successfully achieving the goals of the team. Most important, highly successful teams understand and value how each piece must be aligned to support the whole. In the course of doing this they learn how to support each other and the board as a whole.

> A high-performing trustee knows that excellence in governance requires purposeful action.

How can an ordinary person come onto a board and be expected to develop this governance mindset? The answer is simple. Everyone has the capacity to develop this perspective; the issue is whether they even know and understand the importance of developing it. It is not something that most people know, and it is not automatically intuitive. But it is imminently possible to achieve once you become aware of its critical importance. In other words, the governance mindset is learnable. Incidentally, mindset is akin to *nuance*—the subject of Fullan's (2019) new book.

Systems Thinking in Action
School District, Northern California

This school board had virtually everything going against it. The district had suffered severe financial crisis caused by both state and federal cutbacks and had experienced fraud within the district. Federal officials had investigated, and charges had been filed. The board was turned out, and a new board came in on a recall election. This new board was faced with severe organizational and financial challenges. They were all rookies with no previous board experience. As would be expected, there was stress among the trustees. The person who quickly developed a governance mindset and emerged as the real leader was a woman with no higher education and no professional education expertise. She was the sole owner of a small house cleaning service. It was she who became a highly effective board president. She understood the board could be effective only if they worked together and worried when they didn't. She understood that the problems were too complex to be solved by individual, personal agendas. That simple fact opened up a whole door of understanding. It also had a positive effect on the staff. The superintendent knew that he could talk to her and that she understood not only the heart of the district and how it ran but also the leadership the board could provide. She was a systems thinker, she had a strategic focus, she was a deep learner, and she always watched her manner.

As an example of her leadership, she reduced the fallout from the board's toxic history, smoothing out remaining issues with some new members of the board. Because of her sensitivities, she was able to moderate and, in some cases, mitigate, potential disputes between trustees and between individual trustees and district staff.

SYSTEMS THINKING

Governance is a systems job. High-performing trustees with a governance mindset are first and foremost systems thinkers.

A few years ago, a very mindful and insightful trustee, Sherry Loofbourrow, who served over 13 years on the Newport Mesa USD school board in Orange County, California, and became President of the California School Boards Association, was at home looking out her window when she saw flames and smoke on the hills not far from her house. The fire was headed toward the area where her house was located. As she watched the fire, she also looked up and noticed news coverage on the same fire on her television. Reporters were reporting on the strategy being adopted by key fire officials as they

observed the fire from a helicopter high overhead. She was struck by the difference in perception from standing at her window and looking at the approaching fire and the report on the television from the high-level fire officials. They were talking about the strategy necessary to defeat the whole fire: issues like what to defend and what to let burn, where to allocate scarce resources that would accomplish the most good. Sherry, looking out the window, was thinking about a simple thing: how do I save my house? What do I need to do to make sure everyone in my family is safe?

What became startlingly clear to her was the difference in the two perspectives. One was operating at a macro, systems level, directing resources; the other, on the fire line, making immediate micro, tactical level decisions to fight the fire. It was an aha moment for Sherry when she realized trustees needed to be in the helicopter making system decisions, not on the fire line fighting fires. The problem is that when putting out fires or otherwise operating in the trenches, the perspective is what is right in front of your eyes. The need is to put out that fire as quickly as possible. That is not the job of governance: that is the job of the experts hired specifically to handle the problem. The last thing they need on the line fighting fires is systems people. Note to superintendents: If you put a fire hose in the hands of a trustee, they will get out of the helicopter and fight the fire.

Systems thinking, as Peter Senge has stated, is about stepping back and seeing patterns. "By its very nature, systems thinking points out inter-dependencies and the need for collaboration" (Senge, 1994, p. 92). The National School Boards Association's *Key Works School Board's Guidebook* provides a good operational definition:

> Actions are not taken in isolation. A systems thinker understands that everything is connected to everything else. The goal of systems thinking is to take those actions that will most positively influence the system as a whole. At the same time, every action has a reaction. That is, each action will produce some desired results and, almost certainly, unintended consequences elsewhere in the system. (National School Boards Association, 2000, p. 3)

Systems thinking should be in the service of "something." Our some-thing is the moral imperative of improving learning for *all students* relative to educational outcomes that will be essential for surviving and thriving in ever more complex global societies. School districts are complex organizations, among the most complex in local government. To govern effectively it is essential to understand how all pieces in the organization connect. Systems thinking is simply connecting the dots. Governance is often a zero-sum game. One policy decision in one area almost always impacts other policies and areas that may appear to be unrelated.

The late Maureen DiMarco was California's first Secretary of Educa-tion and Child Development; she also was a sixteen-year trustee and a former President of the California School Boards Association. She had a clear sense of the importance of a systems mindset in the governance of a highly complex school district. Between 1989 and 1990 she gave the speech below a number of times.

The School District as a Complex System
Maureen DiMarco

Take another look at what a school district and school boards are. In my school district, my colleagues and I were the members of a five-member board of directors of a $190 million annual corpora-tion. We were elected to four-year terms by more than 100,000 stakeholders. We were responsible for 4,500 employees at 67 dif-ferent plants. We negotiated annually with four, count them, four different unions. Our plant managers managed four to five times the number of employees that [private sector] managers manage. We were responsible for 38,000 units of production on an annual basis, but we had a 13-year production cycle, rarely with any of these products staying within our company for the entire length

(Continued)

(Continued)

of time. We had no control over our raw materials. We had to take all of them in the numbers in which they arrived and in the condition in which they arrived, and all of our products went out to the marketplace because we had no back room in which to discard our flawed or damaged merchandise. Incidentally, on the side, we operated the second largest transportation agency in [the] county. We served 22,500 meals a day. We operated, if we were lucky, on a 2 percent to 3 percent fiscal margin. We had more regulations than the worst nightmare of a corporate attorney, and we were required to provide supervision in over 89 languages. (Campbell & Greene, 1994)

What DiMarco described is the reality of every school district: interacting parts that must work together in a seamless fashion to support high-quality instructional programs. A trustee with a governance mindset knows that excellence in governance requires the ability to see and understand all the pieces of the system at work. Peter Senge writes that:

Incorporating systems thinking into your behavior requires what David McCamus, former chairman and CEO of Xerox Canada, calls "peripheral vision": The ability to pay attention to the world as if through a wide angle, not a telephoto lens, so you can see how your actions interrelate with other areas of activity. (Senge, 1994, p. 87)

McCamus offers a great metaphor. A wide-angle lens with strong peripheral vision—the ability to focus on one thing but see the surrounding landscape and understand the impact on everything there.

Faculty at Harvard University in their executive leadership programs teach the importance of systems thinking in governance. Ronald Heifetz at the Harvard Kennedy School of Government often draws upon a metaphor developed at the university to demonstrate the appropriate place for policymakers.

The Dance Floor Is Not the Balcony

Ronald Heifetz
King Hussein bin Talal Senior Lecturer in Public Leadership
Founding Director of the Center for Public Leadership
John F. Kennedy School of Government
Harvard University, Cambridge, MA

Let's say you are dancing in a big ballroom. . . . Most of your attention focuses on your dance partner, and you reserve whatever is left to make sure you don't collide with dancers close by. . . . When someone asks you later about the dance, you exclaim, "The band played great, and the place surged with dancers."

But, if you had gone up to the balcony and looked down on the dance floor, you might have seen a very different picture. You would have noticed all sorts of patterns . . . you might have noticed that when slow music played, only some people danced; when the tempo increased, others stepped onto the floor; and some people never seemed to dance at all. . . . the dancers all clustered at one end of the floor, as far away from the band as possible. . . . You might have reported that participation was sporadic, the band played too loud, and you only danced to fast music.

. . . The only way you can gain both a clearer view of reality and some perspective on the bigger picture is by distancing yourself from the fray. (Heifetz & Linsky, 2002)

The message here is clear. Having a governance mindset means spending most of your time in the balcony or the helicopter getting an aerial macro view of the situation. Only then can a trustee see the complete picture or system. Whenever a board or, more likely, an individual trustee, steps into the fray, a loss of context and perspective is almost certain.

STRATEGIC FOCUS

Governance is a strategic job. Highly effective trustees have a strategic focus.
Perhaps the most important aspect of a governance mindset is the context

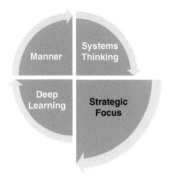

within which trustees govern and the corresponding strategic focus they develop. Context means the conceptual lens through which the trustee views the work of the board. Effective trustees operate from a strategic context rather than a tactical or administrative context. They understand that they are not on the board to administer the organization, but rather to govern it. They understand that governance requires a broad, systemic view
of the district, and they approach all their board responsibilities with a clear focus on achieving the strategic outcomes they have set.

While district staff looks at an issue from an administrative perspective, concentrating on the steps necessary to accomplish an objective or solve a problem, an effective trustee will look at the same issue from a governance perspective, focusing on the impact of that issue on long-term strategic goals, the moral imperative, and organizational and fiscal health of the organization. Understanding this different context of issues, strategic vs. operational or tactical is an extremely important dimension of effective governance.

Many boards fail in accomplishing their governance responsibilities because the individual trustees do not understand the difference between strategic focus and day-to-day administration. While some may understand their role correctly as an individual trustee, they sometimes confuse the application of that role collectively, as a board, thinking that monitoring day-to-day management and approving administrative plans fulfills the board's governance responsibilities. Many trustees have difficulty with the concept of strategy and policy. It seems vague and difficult to define in terms of the practical work of the board. This misunderstanding of a fundamental

> Effective trustees understand that they are not on the board to administer the organization, but rather to govern it.

point often cascades into a series of interventions into administration that often leads to a state of dysfunction by the board.

People often confuse strategic thinking with strategic planning. Strategic thinking refers to the mindset that drives the work of governance. Strategic planning refers to the work of the organization's staff as they develop specific operational goals, projects, and plans to implement the strategic direction set by the governing board and superintendent. Governance is where the moral imperative and the strategic goals of the district live. Strategic focus and systems thinking go hand in hand, and both are a fundamental part of the governance mindset. Strategic thinking needs to be an always present lens through which the governing board and superintendent view the work of the district.

There are three key words for trustees to remember: focus, focus, focus. There are many times when the routine work of the district requires trustees to make incremental, legal, or contract-based decisions. This can challenge even the most mindful trustee to keep focused on the strategic issues. But it is essential that each trustee understand that the value of the board is in the strategic oversight and support that the board provides. What the board brings to the table are the passion, the drive, the commitment to achieve the moral imperative, not distracted by day-to-day administrative challenges. This is purposeful action.

Trustees with a governance mindset understand that questions of implementation should be limited to scheduled oversight reviews or essential discussions, lest administrative issues dominate the board work and push out the strategic work of the board. There is only so much energy and focus in the room during board meetings, and the trustees are going to spend it either on administrative or incremental issues that are tactical in nature or on the big issues and important discussions that keep the organization on track for achieving its strategic goals. In other words, effective trustees spend their time and energy doing their job rather than spending scarce resources on doing the job of those they hired.

The truth is that dealing with administrative problems or issues is much easier than dealing with complex, sometime difficult to comprehend

> The value of the board is in the strategic oversight and support that the board provides. The board brings the passion, the drive, the commitment to achieve the moral imperative, not distracted by day-to-day administrative challenges. This is purposeful action.

educational challenges. Michal Rosenberger, a governance consultant and board trainer observed in her book *Team Leadership: School Boards at Work* (1997):

> The basic human need to overcome feelings of inadequacy encourages trustees to grab hold of issues where they can display some expertise and avoid discussion they don't understand. As they fall into the habit of dealing with organizational, financial, and procedural matters, they neglect their primary function of governing schools.

While a little harsh, Rosenberger reflects the human reality that we all gravitate to those things we understand and tend to avoid those that we do not. It is interesting that a characteristic of a governance mindset is that trustees run toward complexity and depth rather than away from it. From our experience, trustees with a governance mindset when presented with quality information and opportunities for real, authentic discussion, more often than not seriously engage difficult education issues because they represent the real work of the board and in many ways what they signed up for. The common theme of the governance mindset is not only understanding but also embracing the strategic discussions necessary to realizing the moral imperative. Perhaps most of all those trustees who become more effective are willing to go outside their comfort zone to gain new understanding. In a word, they are *learners*.

The greatest enemy of strategic thinking and the powerful policy-making role of boards is the linear, incremental-based board agenda. Trustees must control their agenda and not let their agenda control them. The most common complaint is that board agendas are not focused on children's issues but rather on administrative work. It does not have to be that way. There are many examples of policy or strategic goal-based agendas that are designed to keep the board discussions focused on the important work of the board and minimize the distractions into administrative issues. The importance of this should not be underestimated. By their nature, public board meetings—those regulated by open meeting laws in particular—tend to be driven by tightly developed agendas providing little opportunity for deeper strategic discussions.

DEEP LEARNING

Governance is a job that requires a deep understanding of the issues under-
lying the moral imperative, system-wide coherence, and strategic goals.

Trustees with a governance mindset are committed to making decisions based on quality information, evidence, and data. Effective trustees do
their homework. Trustees realize their governance power through their knowledge and deep
understanding of the issues surrounding the moral
imperative. It is not possible to provide the kind
of strategic direction in education without trustees
coming to every board meeting fully prepared. Vet-
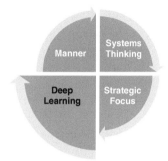
eran trustees often cite lack of preparation and understanding as one of the
most significant characteristics of ineffective trustees.

This particular point in history puts new, more complex demands on
trustees. Deep learning by trustees of the major educational issues in the
21st century requires understanding the challenges facing the students
they serve. As strange as it may sound, becoming literate and numerate
and graduating from high school or even a post-secondary institution is
no longer sufficient for living effectively in the complex, unpredictable
and in many ways dangerous society that is evident. Put another way,
if you are good at academic schooling, are you automatically good at
life? The global competencies and skills required for living in a complex and unpredictable world are not being taught in very many schools.
Every student needs to learn that technology, robots, and artificial intelligence radically change the nature and size of the job market; that climate
change, world conflict, and other factors paint an ominous future; and
that the equity gap in education and life portends a growing ever wider
threat to the fabric of society in terms of trust and social cohesion. In
the current climate, trustees have to understand major innovations in
learning outcomes, teaching and learning, nature of leadership, and the
explosion of new, proactive roles of parents, teachers, and especially
of students as change agents. Introducing and managing fundamental
innovations is difficult at the best of times but is downright perplexing

under conditions of societal uncertainty. We will need trustees to be in the thick of deciding on, and monitoring, the deep learning changes that are essential in the present for the future.

Trustees need to understand that in their schools deep learning happens when all students—regardless of background—become literate and numerate and graduate with strong basic skills. But more than that, deep learning includes global competencies that are crucial for surviving and thriving in a world that gets more complex virtually every day. These are skills such as character, citizenship, collaboration, communication, creativity, and critical thinking. These are the 6Cs that Fullan and his colleagues are helping to implement in partnership with over 1,000 schools in 8 different countries (Fullan, Quinn, & McEachen, 2018; see Figure 2.1).

It is easy to say trustees should be informed, up to date, and knowledgeable about the many issues about which they make decisions. However, access to quality data is a major challenge on many boards. Lack of data or evidence to support policy and decision making is the Achilles heel of governance. How much information does a board need, how often, and, most important, what kind or type of information is appropriate for making policy and oversight decisions?

The issue of deep learning by trustees in governance goes to the heart of the board's support and ownership of district-wide coherence making. Are boards the owners of the educational program in the district or simply the audience? Is the administration only informing the board, usually with a polished PowerPoint presentation, or are they engaging the board? As Doug Eadie states,

> If you want someone or some entity like a board to feel like the owner of a course of action, a product, a decision—of anything— you must get them involved in generating or shaping that course, product or decision, rather than merely reacting to your best thinking. (Eadie, 2003, p. 31)

What we all know is that in adult learning engagement is essential. It requires a deep dive into the theory, the "why," behind the major programs enacted to achieve the moral imperative. Most important, engagement requires open and authentic discussion and dialogue.

Figure 2.1 **Global Competencies for Learning: The 6Cs**

	Character
	Proactive stance toward life and learning to learn
	• Grit, tenacity, perseverance, and resilience • Empathy, compassion, and integrity in action
	Citizenship
	A global perspective
	• Commitment to human equity and well-being through empathy and compassion for diverse values and world views • Genuine interest in human and environmental sustainability • Solving ambiguous and complex problems in the real world to benefit citizens
	Collaboration
	Working interdependently as a team
	• Interpersonal and team-related skills • Social, emotional, and intercultural skills • Managing team dynamics and challenges
	Communication
	Communication designed for audience and impact
	• Message advocates a purpose and makes an impact • Reflection to further develop and improve communication • Voice and identity expressed to advance humanity
	Creativity
	Economic and social entrepreneurialism
	• Asking the right inquiry questions • Pursuing and expressing novel ideas and solutions • Leadership to turn ideas into action
	Critical Thinking
	Evaluating information and arguments
	• Making connections and identifying patterns • Constructing meaningful knowledge • Experimenting, reflecting, and taking action on ideas in the real world

Part of the challenge for a trustee is that no one can know everything. Looking back at DiMarco's description of her district, how can a trustee have deep knowledge about transportation, food services, health care, facilities, construction, as well as finance and budget and, most important, curriculum and instruction? The answer lies in strategic focus. Deep learning should focus on the few, maybe three or four, major strategic goals tied to the moral imperative. And for those priorities, the superintendent and trustees should be locked into an ongoing review and reporting system, so both governance and administration are current and on the same track.

The primary source of information for supporting board action is, of course, the superintendent and staff of the district. It is essential that trustees trust and have confidence in the quality and validity of this information. If a trustee does not totally trust information from the superintendent and/or senior staff, serious doubts are raised that can begin to erode confidence in the overall administration of the district. Much of the discord and distrust on a board can be traced to a lack of confidence in the quality of the information provided to the board by the staff. This lack of confidence in turn might cause the trustee to look for alternative sources of information. Trustees who go down this road can get caught in a downward cycle of mistrust. This can lead to a toxic governance environment that can undermine the effectiveness of the entire board.

If doubt over the quality of information provided by staff begins to form, it is essential that steps be taken to address the concerns before they contaminate the overall governance culture of the board. Any trustee who begins to feel a lack of confidence needs to engage both the board president and the superintendent in an honest exchange to address the source of the mistrust and, it is to be hoped, reach a resolution. An alternative course, depending upon the culture of the board, is to engage the entire board in a discussion regarding the issue. As things stand, too many boards don't really know the focus and climate of their schools. Our theme throughout this book is that being informed, focused, and engaged is a mutual endeavor of trustees and superintendents.

The problem often is not that trustees do not have access to information about the district programs. The reality is that trustees are constantly bombarded with information. As Rosenberger (1997) says, "It is unrealistic to expect trustees not to be learning about the school through informal means. Trustees are still members of the community hearing things from their children, family members, and constituents" (p. 62). The challenge is how that information fits with the information from the district. Great care must be taken by trustees at these times to understand that, as in the case of informal staff input, they are hearing only one side of every story. For trustees with a governance mindset, their greatest strength in these exchanges is their deep understanding of the purpose and work of the district.

One of a trustee's most valuable activities is to take the time to visit schools. A well-organized, well-intentioned visit will often benefit both the trustee and the staff. For the staff, it is an opportunity to see the trustee in a setting other than a formal board meeting. It is a time when relationships can be established or strengthened and when staff members can be appreciated and supported by the trustee. For the trustee, it's an opportunity to learn important information about the internal operation of the organization as well as a chance to get to know the staff on a more informal basis. It is also a chance to see the programs the board has approved in action.

For these visits to be successful and a benefit to the board and staff, it is essential that the tone of the visit be positive and well coordinated and that trustees understand that informal information from staff in these settings should be carefully assessed and no judgments made on the spot. There are occasions when trustee school site visits can become a problem. Whenever a trustee "drops by" for a quick, unannounced visit, almost nothing good can ever happen. Staff are not prepared, may be in the middle of a difficult task, or involved in stressful situations where imposition of a trustee is the last thing they need. What is particularly tenuous is when a trustee is on a mission to discover information regarding a specific issue and is trolling for information among an unsuspecting staff. Usually this occurs because of a lack of trust or confidence by the trustee in the senior staff of the organization. For whatever reason, such trustees are convinced that unedited information from alternative levels of administration will be more truthful. Rather than take this course, the board should collectively discuss strategies for addressing credibility concerns among the staff that don't involve making surreptitious visits that undermine trust and the culture of collaboration. Strategies that reinforce openness, teamwork, and trust will be much more beneficial to the board in the long run.

MANNER

- Shake not the head, feet, or legs. Roll not the eyes, lift not one eyebrow higher than the other.

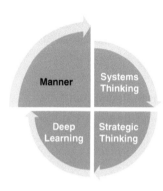

  - Turn not your back to others, especially in speaking. Jog not the table or desk on which another reads or writes. Lean not upon anyone.

  - Speak not injurious words, neither in jest nor earnest. Scoff at no one, although they give occasion.

  - Undertake not what you cannot perform. Be careful to keep your promises.

- Speak not evil of those who are absent, for it is unjust.

- Be not tedious in discourse; make not many digressions; nor repeat often the same manner of discourse. (George Washington, Rules of Civility, 1745)

We said earlier that manner seems rather curious in a set of concepts for core change. Yet little things can mean a lot. Change is about relationships and a trustee's manner can erode or build trust. A poor public manner by trustees, even if unintentional, can turn the climate sour. At a recent governance workshop with relatively new trustees, trustees were asked a few questions:

1. When thinking about public or private leaders whom you admire and respect and when they left their professional positions, left a

very positive legacy, what were the main characteristics of their leadership?

What was it about them that led to such success as a leader?

The answers that came back were always consistent:

Visionary, listener, courageous, consensus builder, ethical, wise

These were serious responses, not attempting to be politically correct. These were the characteristics that were appreciated by the audience.

Then on another sheet of paper, a second question was asked:

2. What about leaders who left negative legacies, leaders who people could not wait until they left their office or board?

The answers here were even quicker and more consistent:

Arrogant, dominating, manipulative, unethical, dishonest, divider

These too were serious responses, even more emotional and definitive than the positive.

Finally, a third question was asked:

3. Which list are you on?

This always caused pause and extended silence. The follow-up question: Do you think that when the people you thought of as ineffective and negative got up in the morning, looked in the mirror and said, "Today I am going to be arrogant, dishonest, and dominating"? Probably not. So, what is going on here? These are perceptions caused by the behaviors chosen by these individuals. Are they truly dishonest? Maybe. Are they acting arrogantly? Maybe. It is true that some great leaders have displayed characteristics from both lists. The important question, and the one answered by the audience, is "What characteristics define them and their leadership?" What profile defines them on a consistent basis? Therein defines the positive or negative legacies that await them.

The point here is that the successes of any leaders—anyone in power and authority—no matter how big or small their office, are determined in large part by the manner in which they carry out their leadership. While perceptions of others cannot be controlled, individual trustees (and superintendents) can choose to act in a manner that reflects their internal compass and core beliefs and not in a way that creates perceptions and reactions that are negative and counterproductive to achieving their goals.

> The successes of any leaders are determined in large part by the manner in which they carry out their leadership. One of the most important and often least appreciated traits of highly effective trustees is management of their public behavior.

One of the most important and often least appreciated traits of highly effective trustees is management of their public behavior. Trustees with a governance mindset always mind their manner. They understand that working toward common ground and strategic goals with other independently elected or appointed trustees in a collaborative setting requires patience, understanding, respect, common courtesy, and, most important, a sense of humor. Such trustees model civic behavior and understand that how they govern as an individual is often more critical than what they say or do. Above all, they are very conscious of modeling the behavior they want the children in the district to emulate.

When sitting at the board table, individual trustees are operating in a fishbowl. Everyone is watching. Their words, body language, and tone of voice define the message they are communicating. Dr. Albert Mehrabian, a UCLA professor, has developed data on the relative importance of verbal and nonverbal communication. As seen in the pie chart in Figure 2.2, words count for only 7% of the content received in a communication, while voice tonality and body language count for 93% (Mulder, 2012). Carl W. Buehner is quoted as having said, "They may forget what you said—but they will never forget how you made them feel."

We intuitively know this to be true. Think about the reaction to someone who enters the room with a smile and happy expression and exclaims in a happy voice "Good morning!!" We know this person is off to a good day. On the other hand, visualize the same person entering the room with a frown, downcast, tired look, who quietly mutters, "Good morning." The same words with a completely different tone and body language result in

Figure 2.2 **Communication Is Both Verbal and Nonverbal**

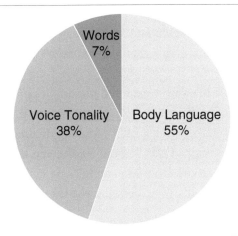

Source: Mulder (2012)

a very different impression. We read into these behaviors, tones, and body language entirely different messages. Trustees with a governance mindset tend to be very self-aware of their own manner and personal style of communication. They understand that the only behavior they can control is their own.

The problem for many trustees is that while they recognize negative behavior in others, they often don't see the same behavior in themselves. In the legacy exercise rarely would any trustee when asked, see herself or himself on the negative list. Most people are not aware of how they come across to others. One way to find out is ask a family member, friend, or colleague to tape the board meeting—without sound. Just watch yourself at the board table, watch mannerisms, how you respond while others are talking. This is how the community or your district staff sees you.

In some instances, judgments are made from observing physical facial characteristics or intense, thoughtful expressions. At the height of a particularly interesting conversation, lecture, or seminar, it is easy to look out over the participants and pick out people who look stern, off-putting, and sometimes even angry. The person may be just thinking intently about the conversation or issue unaware of the image he or she is projecting. Add to this that often the tone used in making comments might enhance what could become a negative assessment of the individual. At the board table and from the audience, this can create a mistaken judgment regarding not only the person's point of view but also the overall person.

It is not possible to overestimate the importance of high-quality communication to an effective trustee. A trustee with a governance mindset understands that communication, both speaking and listening, is the core of governance leadership. Deep learning gives the trustee the depth of understanding necessary to lead. Managing their manner and developing their communication skills give them the ability to use that learning in a positive and purposeful way.

"The single biggest problem in communication is the illusion that it has taken place." *(often attributed to George Bernard Shaw)*

While acknowledging that cultural differences play a part in miscommunication and the percentages used in the pie chart can be argued, there can be no question that voice tone and body language have a huge impact on communication. How many times has someone said, "That's not what I meant" when observing the reaction to some statement or comment? All people in relationships understand the concept of intent versus impact all too well.

Among communication and leadership professionals, the concept of intent vs. impact is commonly used to demonstrate the dynamics of interpersonal communication.

For trustees this is a huge issue. What do trustees do? They talk. They communicate. And as a board, they must communicate in a public setting. There are two parts to communication. Speaking and listening. In many ways listening skills are as important or even more important. Whether at the board table or in the supermarket, trustees communicate. The foundation of effective communication is first to listen. The late Stephen Covey is among the most quoted leadership experts in the country. He wrote about the importance of empathic listening.

When I say empathic listening, I mean listening with intent to understand. I mean seeking first to understand, to really understand. It's an entirely different paradigm. Empathic (from empathy) listening gets inside another person's frame of reference. You look out through it, you see the world the way they see the world, you understand their paradigm, you understand how they feel. (Covey, 2017, p. 252)

Much of what Covey refers to as empathic listening is about using more than the functional use of ears. It is interesting that the Chinese symbol of listening incorporates the symbols for these elements: you, ear, eyes, undivided attention, and heart (see Figure 2.3). That says it all.

Figure 2.3   **Chinese Listening Symbol**

The Chinese characters that make up the verb "to listen" tell us something significant about this skill.

To Listen

YOU

EAR

EYES

UNDIVIDED
ATTENTION

HEART

CONCLUDING COMMENTS

Is there a secret sauce to effective governance? The closest we have found is in the wisdom inherent in the governance mindset. The role of school trustee is more complicated, more important than it first might have appeared, and more positively exciting when done well. It involves sorting out and developing your own governance mindset, and doing so in relation to others (your fellow trustees, the superintendent, the staff) all at the same time. We believe that the organizers and themes in this book will make this sorting and synergy work easier and more powerful, and in the end much more efficacious for education and society as a whole. The timing is crucial. More changes must and will be managed in the next few years than has been the case in the last decade. It is time to be at your governance best.

3

Superintendent Governance Mindset

· ·

If anything goes bad, I did it.
If anything goes semi-good, then we did it.
If anything goes real good, then you did it.
That's all it takes to get people to win football games.

—Legendary University of Alabama Coach
Paul "Bear" Bryant (Williams, 2010)

t's not just high-performing trustees who govern with a well-developed governance mindset; effective superintendents do so as well. Some superintendents make matters worse for their districts (and themselves) by neglecting to think enough about the crucial governance function of the system. Since superintendents are key supporters as well as partners with boards in their governance work, it is important that superintendents understand the principles of effective governance as well as they do curriculum and instruction and administration. However, many superintendents simply view the board as an external power source, important and legitimate but not a part of the superintendent's team. They do not view the board as a critical piece of the education puzzle that needs to be addressed by them in a strategic way. This is really not surprising since there is virtually nothing to prepare a superintendent for governance. Even going to board meetings for years does not fully prepare a superintendent for the reality of working with an elected governing board.

A new superintendent had just been appointed to a school district in California. During a lunch discussion, the question of his initial plans for the district came up. He was an excellent superintendent, a great educator, and a genuinely good person. He was so excited to share his ideas. He had a plan for the principals, for the teachers and their union, for the parents and community engagement, and of course for the instructional program. When he finished, there was silence. And then came the question,

"And?"

Surprised, he replied, "And what?"

"What about your board? What is your plan for the board?"

He looked puzzled and said, "Why would I need a plan for the board? I work for the board."

His perspective is quite common among superintendents. It is only natural, but alas not productive, that people tend to plan for those things they perceive they have control over — neglecting other more complex matters that they need to resolve.

These more complex matters include:

- What governance styles do superintendents typically use?
- How do successful superintendents approach governance?
- What is entailed in supporting a trustee governance mindset?

TYPICAL GOVERNANCE STYLES

Over the years as superintendents gain experience, they develop a personal and professional perspective on governance and boards based on the experiences they have had in their districts. It is possible to cluster governance styles of superintendents into three broad categories. These are Hands Off, Preemptive Damage Control, and Purposeful.

Hands Off Approach

Many superintendents adopt a hands-off perspective with the board. That is, superintendents believe that attempting to help boards in the governance process is not their responsibility and can only lead to charges of manipulation and attempting to manage the board. They don't feel they have much time to spend with the board; they believe it's their job to run the district, not to worry about the board. These superintendents tend to admire and envy superintendents with the shortest possible board meetings and adhere to the often-stated adage that the most important thing is for the board to appoint the superintendent and then stay out of his or her way.

This approach actually presumes the superintendent has no governance responsibilities. At a national meeting on urban education a number of years ago, a prominent superintendent voiced this very point of view. He believed that the board was the board, whatever it turned out to be and it was not appropriate for him to get involved "in their work." The danger in adopting this approach is that as gaps between governance and administration begin to widen—as they most assuredly will—the superintendent in all probability will not have the relationship, confidence, and trust necessary to bridge the gap.

Preemptive Damage Control Approach

Another view is that the best way to deal with boards is to keep them in the dark. These superintendents believe their primary job is to protect the staff from the board and to keep the board out of the work of the district. These superintendents tend to focus on the "care and feeding of the board" and keep tight control over anything that affects the board's operation. They ensure that agendas are carefully constructed to focus on easy-to-handle, often administrative, matters that will not cause a significant problem in the district one way or the other. They control all staff contacts with the board. Interestingly, in some cases it's almost as if the roles have shifted. The strategic direction is set by the superintendent while the board focuses on small-scale, day-to-day administrative issues.

Purposeful Approach

There is a third way that superintendents approach governance in their district. It is not coincidental that superintendents who have long, productive tenures, some with large complex districts, approach governance in a thoughtful, analytical, and purposeful manner. They develop their own governance mindset. It is not that they are better educators than other superintendents (although they may very well be); it's that they approach governance as a key function of the district. Not as something to control or ignore, but something to support as a critical part of the education system.

As Paul Houston, the former executive Director of the American Association of School Administrators (AASA) and Doug Eadie, a nationally known expert on school governance, write:

> One of your primary responsibilities as superintendent and CEO of your district is to play a leading role in building and maintaining strategically significant relationships, and the one that is at the heart of your district's strategic policy-level leadership—and most critical to your effectiveness as CEO— is between you and your school board. (Houston & Eadie, 2002, p. 73)

They also say that the superintendent "views his or her partnership with the board as a precious and fragile bond that can be easily broken if not conscientiously and continuously maintained" (p. 13).

A great example of the proactive superintendent in action is from a school district in California. Identifying behavior patterns to get to "Yes!" is the story of a purposeful superintendent's strategy to build governance support for a major district initiative.

Being purposeful in governance means making it one of the superintendent's highest priorities.

Identifying Behavior Patterns to Get to "Yes!"
Anonymous, Superintendent
California School District

One of the greatest challenges to coherence is when a superintendent is working with stakeholders and the governing board to implement a major change in curriculum to improve instructional outcomes for students. Equally challenging is navigating the competing interests trustees face from various stakeholders including teachers, site leaders, and the community. Recently, an urban district in California faced and overcame such challenges when systemically implementing a targeted initiative rooted in student data. While the data generated was from students in classrooms, moving the initiative forward was grounded in the relational capital built over several years working with district stakeholders, and, most important, the governing board. Valuing the learning from these relationships allowed the superintendent and staff to think differently, adjust approaches, and get the district to "Yes!"

With math results flat—only 24% of students meeting or exceeding state standard proficiency, there was an urgent need to change math instruction. Taking learning from an intentional network of present and past superintendents throughout the state, the superintendent sought an opportunity with a professional development company. The company offered a lesson design that supported standards and pedagogy and provided staff with ongoing assistance in their classrooms, with the students. Even with this support, the district raced against time. Knowing the students could not wait another year, a quick decision was necessary, leading to a short timeline of implementation of new materials, making traditional models of adopting curriculum not possible. Key stakeholders and some trustees had mixed feelings about this approach. The 4th year superintendent relied on the relationships built over time to accomplish the task.

The superintendent understood that purposeful action was needed for the board to fully understand the urgency and opportunity available through the proposed initiative. In order to provide a deep dive

(Continued)

(Continued)

into the program and respect the differing learning styles of trustees, the superintendent held individual meetings with each board member to process the assessment results and to discuss what the results meant for the students of the district. Further, the superintendent listened to the concerns of each board member to better understand their perspective. Staff provided additional information by engaging the board during regular board meetings to introduce the curricular initiative and the potential it presented for the district. These efforts resulted in the board approving this intense math initiative by unanimous vote. Although this was a huge success, it was only the beginning of the efforts needed to allow the implementation of the initiative to succeed.

Within a month of implementation, a vocal minority of original critics of the program, including some staff, continuously fed negative information to the board. During this time the superintendent and program staff continued to keep the board up to date, stressing the data and the lack of success the students were experiencing in the current math program while presenting the successes the company had accomplished in similar districts. Opportunities for positive teacher and leader voices to be heard were created, particularly those who were less vocal but supported the implementation and were experiencing early successes with students. Trustees were dealing with competing information, and it was apparent that without experiencing compelling evidence, the district could lose an excellent opportunity to support students and teachers.

Using knowledge of specific board dynamics, the superintendent shifted the approach during implementation. It was decided to involve individual trustees where the action is—the classroom—in order to directly address the negative perceptions of the program. The goal was to allow them to see the instruction in action and hear from teachers and students. As a result, hearing the positive impact the program was having directly from students and teachers began to drown the voices of opposition. The influence of board members who had experienced the program firsthand became more compelling than the opinions of naysayers.

The results of the implementation in the first year of the initiative was a district-wide increase of 3% in math student achievement. These results were promising. In subsequent years, as more and more teachers embraced implementation and grew in their capacity to provide math instruction to the students of the district, even higher results were expected.

From both a systems and strategic perspective, highly successful superintendents understand and act in a way that reinforces their recognition of governance as both a necessity and an asset to district-wide coherence. Being purposeful takes time and energy, something that superintendents with a governance mindset understand. As Houston and Eadie put it:

> Highly successful superintendents act in a way that reinforces their recognition of governance as both a necessity and an asset to district-wide coherence.

> Putting governance on your short list of top priorities means that your board is always a giant blip on your CEO radar screen. It means that you allocate significant time and detailed attention to board affairs, that you become a true expert in this complex, evolving field, and that you make a strong commitment to board capacity building. (2002, p. 15)

Once deciding to take a purposeful, proactive role with the board, the superintendent must address a number of issues. A superintendent's governance mindset requires a deep understanding of the governance function and what the superintendent needs to do to ensure that a positive governance system is established.

EXAMPLES OF PURPOSEFUL SUPERINTENDENT SUPPORT FOR GOVERNANCE

Notwithstanding the perception about the "revolving door" of superintendents, there are numerous examples of high-achieving districts with long-tenured superintendents. We have chosen three districts in California, one in the state of Washington, and one in South Carolina to examine the role of the purposeful superintendent. All five districts have both high levels of at-risk children and at the same time have been recognized for high performance.

Superintendent Chris Steinhauser
Long Beach Unified School District, California

Long Beach Unified School District is the third largest school district in California, with 75,000 students, 68% of whom are eligible for free and reduced-price lunches. Long Beach received the national Broad Prize for Urban Education in 2003 and has qualified as a finalist for the award five times. In a 2010 report, McKinsey & Company named the Long Beach Unified School District one of the world's 20 leading school systems—and one of the top three in the United States.

Chris Steinhauser is completing his 16th year as superintendent of Long Beach. His predecessor, Carl Cohn, a highly respected educator, served as superintendent for ten years. Superintendents prior to that served equally long tenures. Steinhauser attributes his long-term success in governance to a culture of trust and respect that exists among the board and between the board and staff. One of Steinhauser's core governance beliefs is that "you must never violate that trust." He believes that part of that trust comes from open and authentic communication with and among trustees. For example, Steinhauser has a rule that no trustee will ever read something in the newspaper without hearing about it from him first.

But most important, Steinhauser has ensured that the board deeply understands the purpose and work of the district, and that the board shares a moral purpose that is present up and down the district. Steinhauser has taken concrete steps to engage the board in deep learning, and as a result the board is always up to date on the key strategic issues. For example, the board schedules three full-day retreats a year. In these sessions, the board "deep dives," as Steinhauser describes it, into the work of the district. This ensures that each trustee not only is informed but also develops an understanding of the "why" of each program. These retreats are well attended by the board, usually at 100%.

The board governs through the use of board committees where major substantive issues are discussed. While not uncommon for larger districts, the use of committees in Long Beach plays a purposeful governance function. Trustees are expected to participate and provide advice and counsel, and most important to keep the full board informed and up to date on major issues.

Superintendent Laura Schwalm (retired)
Garden Grove Unified School District, California

Garden Grove Unified School District in Orange County, California, is a large district with 48,000 students, 68% qualifying for free and reduced-price lunches. Garden Grove is recognized as a top district both in California and nationally, receiving the Broad Prize in 2004. Recently retired after 14 years as superintendent of Garden Grove, Schwalm makes it clear that a major factor in her success can be attributed to a purposeful, highly proactive relationship with the board. During her tenure with the district she worked closely with the board, making sure they owned the instructional program. She believed that the secret to the relationship was that she always tried to give the board credit for the major accomplishments of the district. She also always made sure they knew she was supporting them, "watching their back." She made sure that each trustee was fully informed on all the programs and was presented with information in a way that would help them communicate with the community. She was conscious of their perspectives and of the pressures they felt as elected officials.

Schwalm was always honest, straightforward, and purposeful. Her internal moral compass was to be very visible. She made a remarkable statement that reflected both her values and her nonnegotiable position as superintendent:

(*Continued*)

(Continued)

> I came to this work to make a difference for children, and sometimes in the superintendency you can start feeling far from that. To keep that at the forefront of my mind, and to help get through the difficult times that always come, I would remind myself that while I was now accountable to the board, I still worked for the children, just as I did when I was a teacher.

Superintendent Marc Johnson (retired)
Sanger Unified School District, California

Sanger Unified School District is located in the Central Valley of California, one of the prime agricultural regions in the country. The district has 76% of students qualifying for free and reduced-price lunches. Sanger has a seven-member board of trustees. Marc Johnson recently retired after serving for 11 years as superintendent. In 2011 Johnson received the National Superintendent of the Year Award from the American Association of School Administrators.

When Johnson took over as superintendent, the district had serious problems with both governance and the educational program. He was extremely fortunate early on to have a very strong board president. They understood that a new board mindset was needed. One of their first tasks was to establish a governance structure with emphasis on protocols and norms.

Johnson established a practice to assure that prior to any action, the board was fully engaged and informed. He always made sure the board understood the "why" of a program before they were asked for approval. In-depth briefings before votes were held, and if the staff team felt the board didn't agree or that they didn't understand, they would not hesitate to hit the pause button. They did not care that much about getting a 7-0 vote; it was more important that the board understood.

Most important, Johnson made a commitment to keep children at the forefront of everything. He surrounded the board with data and program information on how the children were doing at all times. When asked the two most important steps he took to engage the board in the work of the district, Johnson gave two examples. First, during the school year, they held structured school site visits for the board. These were not just casual visits; they were designed as a learning tool to show the board how the programs they approved were being implemented in real time with real children.

Second, one decision that Johnson believes had major positive effects on governance was to have sit-down dinner meetings with the board and the superintendent's cabinet and other senior staff one hour before every board meeting. While it is not uncommon for boards to have meals before a board meeting, Sanger's approach was different. These dinners were structured for interaction. This was a time for serious conversation, allowing trustees and staff to visit and build relationships with one another. When possible, as a strategy, Johnson would try to pair staff members and trustees who liked each other and were compatible.

Johnson felt the most important thing a superintendent should do is always be honest with the board. "Never try and hide from the board; a superintendent should never try to fake their way through a problem." Second, while Johnson felt it important to build relationships with the board, he believed that this should always be secondary to keeping children as the highest priority.

Finally, when asked what the biggest mistake a superintendent can make with the board, Johnson was adamant. "Never lie to the board, either by misinformation or by omission." He believes some superintendents present only half the story and give the board a false perception of reality; "You must confront the ugly," he emphasizes.

Superintendent Steven Webb
Vancouver Public Schools, Washington State

Vancouver Public Schools is located in southern Washington State on the border with Oregon. The district has 24,000 students with 48% eligible for free and reduced-price lunches. Steve Webb has served as superintendent of the district for 11 years. He was the 2016 Washington State Superintendent of the Year and was one of four finalists for the 2016 National Superintendent of the Year. Under his administration, the district experienced significant improvement in kindergarten literacy, a 20-point decrease in the 3rd grade English Language Learner Literacy gap, and a 180% increase in the percentage of students in poverty enrolled in Advanced Placement (AP)/ International Baccalaureate (IB) as examples of their strategic focus.

Webb emphasized the importance of the board in the district's accomplishments. "Boards have a legitimate role in the way the school district functions." He stated, "These six relationships (five board members plus Webb) are critical to shaping the future of the district." He believes that his extensive work with the board accounts for much of his success as a superintendent. Webb listed three main reasons for the positive governance system in the district:

1. Timely two-way communication and authentic engagement with the board

2. Board commitment to internal and external public engagement in cultivating a hopeful vision

3. Agreement on governance team values, expectations, norms, and protocols (rules of engagement) and focused evaluations on the way the governance team functions

He described his board as fully engaged with the district's strategic agenda. The district has six strategic goals, and most of the work of the board is centered on these goals. A one-hour work session is scheduled before each board meeting. These sessions primarily focus on the six strategic goals. Every quarter a more detailed work session, usually two hours, is scheduled to focus in more detail on the strategic goals.

Superintendent W. Burke Royster
Greenville County Schools, South Carolina

Greenville County Schools, with 76,000 students, is the largest district in in South Carolina. Fifty-one percent of its students qualify for free and reduced-price lunches. Royster has been superintendent of Greenville County Schools for 7 years. Prior to his appointment he served as Deputy Superintendent in the district for 7 years. Royster was named 2018 South Carolina Superintendent of the Year. The district has recorded impressive improvements in most South Carolina accountability measures. One major initiative is Graduation Plus, which has resulted in major increases in graduation rates, particularly in the minority student population and in the number of students graduating with college credits, industry certifications, or both. In giving recognition for the success, Royster stated:

> The improvement in our report rating mirrors enhancements across the district in instructional delivery, student engagement, and rigor. It also reflects the extremely supportive and visionary leadership of our Board of Trustees and the commitment and dedication of our principals, teachers, administrators, and staff.

Greenville County Schools has a 12-member board of trustees. Many of members of the board are long serving. Royster is very analytical in his approach to the board and its governance role. He believes in the importance of keeping the board fully informed and engaged with "truthful information." Royster makes the point that even in cases where he is not required to get approval from the board, he will often involve the board around potential actions he or the staff might take. His goal is to make sure the board never hears about a program or issue from someone else. No surprises. If the board does make a decision, Royster will always make sure the board members know the background ahead of time before they have to act.

Royster stated that he always stresses with his staff that governance "is chess, not checkers." He wants everyone to be thinking

(Continued)

(Continued)

three moves ahead, looking beyond what is most immediately before them. He believes strongly that where possible trustees need to have information tailored to their own learning style. Most important, the board must have confidence in the information it receives.

WHAT THESE SUPERINTENDENTS HAVE IN COMMON

So what do these high-performing superintendents have in common? What can we learn from their governance success? For one thing, they are all smart, deep thinkers and learners. Successful superintendents are purposeful, have a well-developed internal moral compass, and are extremely focused.

Purposeful

Perhaps the most significant characteristic of all five superintendents is that they are extremely purposeful in their work with their boards. It is clear that they see governance as an integral and essential part of the work of the district. These superintendents are analytical, consistent, and coherent in their work with the board. They have a strategy to support governance, are transparent about it, and implement it in a consistent manner. It is not surprising that successful districts, such as the ones we have been discussing, often become well known for the quality of their superintendents. Rarely are their *school boards* by themselves cited as the source of success. Our conclusion in this book is that districts beget success because of the quality of their core governance. Trustees and superintendents working together!

> These five superintendents are extremely purposeful in their work with their boards. They see governance as an integral and essential part of the work of the district.

All of these superintendents developed strategies to engage their boards and involve them in the strategic goals of the district. Chris Steinhauser with his three annual deep-dive retreats, Marc Johnson with the structured on-site visits and pre-board dinners, and Steve Webb with the hourly strategic discussions before every board meeting are just a few examples of creative and effective ways to develop deep understanding and ownership by the board of the district's strategic direction. What is apparent in all five districts is that despite the complexity and challenges of these districts, all five boards have developed trust and confidence in their superintendents.

Internal Moral Compass

One of the things that jumps out when observing the five superintendents who have forged long-term relationships with their boards is they all have deep, well-developed, and authentic internal moral compasses. These superintendents have a clear picture of where they are going and have a deep understanding of how to get there. They are also committed to having their board on that journey with them.

Not surprisingly, the trustees in these districts developed a high level of respect and belief in the competency and effectiveness of these super-intendents. Trust comes from the belief that the superintendent will do the right thing for the right reasons. Interestingly, at no time in any of the con-versations with these superintendents was micromanagement mentioned. All the board trainings and exhortations against micromanagement and dysfunction will never replace a board's belief in the honesty, competency, and moral purpose of their superintendent.

The superintendent builds a relationship that is based on transparent, authentic belief systems. Successful superintendents do not "spin" the information given to the board. They give the good and the bad and don't try to manipulate the information. They don't hide mistakes, nor do they claim all victories. The powerful and deeply held conviction of all five superintendents to the core value of truthfulness, openness and authentic-ity, has a profound effect on the superintendent board relationship.

Marc Johnson's "You must never lie to the board either overtly or by omission," Steinhauser's "you must never violate that trust," and Royster's importance of "truthful information" all reflect that deep-seated belief in the importance of authenticity and transparency in their partnership with the board. These superintendents meet the definition of highly success-ful CEOs in Jim Collins's description of a "level 5 executive" as a leader that "builds enduring greatness through a paradoxical blend of personal humility and professional will" (2002).

Focus, Focus, Focus

These superintendents are highly focused both in their leadership in the dis-trict and in their governance work with their board. Most important, they are consistent. They understand how damaging shifting beliefs and strategies can be to the governance system. They also understand that focus and consistency in the strategy do not mean a lack of flexibility in implementation. By keeping the board up to date and fully informed and engaged at the systems and strategic level, the superintendent ensures that adaptations of administration during implementation are fully understood and supported.

District-Wide Coherence

Perhaps most important, highly effective superintendents with a governance mindset are committed to developing district-wide coherence and understand the essential need for the board to own that coherence. Coherence making without the deep understanding and commitment of the board is not system-wide coherence. If the board does not share in the understanding of the purpose and work of the district, then that work is vulnerable. It would be impossible to sustain the district work if the board were not an owner of the work and a knowledgeable partner in coherence making. Recall that coherence making is a function of purposeful, authentic, continuous interaction that produces "a shared sense of understanding about the nature of the work." Ongoing focused interaction is critical.

Great Teachers and Facilitators

These superintendents are at their core great teachers and facilitators. They have the ability, as teachers, to motivate, energize, and provide deep learning opportunities to trustees. For example, they view difficult questions, not as micromanagement, but as opportunities to facilitate understanding. They exhibit respect by the way they interact with trustees as a board as well as individuals. Sherry Loofbourrow, former president of the California School Boards Association, noted that what drew her most to her longtime superintendent and close friend, John Nicoll, was that he always listened to her, even if he did not always agree. More important, he *heard* her. Houston and Eadie say it very strongly:

> In our experience, CEOs who build strong, positive, enduring partnerships with their boards are inevitably highly skilled facilitators of process, basically because board involvement in helping generate important outcomes, as we noted earlier, is the only reliable way to turn your board into owners who are strongly committed. (2002, p. 23)

SUPPORTING A TRUSTEE GOVERNANCE MINDSET

Superintendents who have chosen purposeful action in support of board governance have an opportunity to directly support the trustee's governance mindset. There are specific steps the superintendent can take, in fact needs to take, if trustees are to fully develop their governance skills. As we noted in Chapter 2, the governance mindset consists of four components: systems thinking, strategic focus, deep learning, and manner. This applies to the superintendent as well as the trustees and is a creature of their joint interaction and mutual commitment.

Systems Thinking

If we expect trustees to be systems thinkers, it is important for the superintendent to support that mindset by making the big-picture organizational implications clear as part of the ongoing governance work of the board. By framing issues and programs, such as continuous improvement, required innovation, closing the achievement gap, or increasing graduation rates, from a systems perspective, making the district-wide connections and impacts visible to the board, the superintendent supports the development of systems thinking in the board. Using the metaphor of peripheral vision, the superintendent needs to make it clear that decisions made in one area have a both anticipated and unanticipated impact on other parts of the district. This mindset helps keep the board's focus on district-wide impacts rather than only on single, narrow interests. Trustees with a governance mindset understand that the board must address system-wide issues and not be focused on single programs and agendas except as part of an integrated educational program.

Strategic Focus

As we have stated, governance is a strategic job. As keeper of the moral imperative, the mission, vision, and strategic goals, the board's primary job is to keep the governance focus on accomplishing the district's strategic direction. The superintendent has an important role in assisting the board in carrying out these responsibilities.

The first challenge is for the superintendent and board to agree on what is strategic and what is tactical. Unfortunately, the line is not always clear. This is also where the oversight function of the board comes into play. It is in this area that much of the stress and tension in governance can develop. It is also where issues of micromanagement arise. It is absolutely essential that the superintendent and the board have open, clear discussions about the administration-governance relationship. It matters more that there is mutual understanding and agreement with the board than what the specific details are. Defining what is strategic and what is tactical will go a long way in minimizing conflict.

The structure of the board meeting is key to the strategic focus and in many ways reflects the governance culture of the board. Since most boards look to the superintendent and the board chair to structure the public meetings through the agenda-setting process, it is essential that there be an agreement on how to maintain a strategic focus on the work of the district. If a superintendent and board president structure the agendas around operational issues, then the board will respond in kind. If most of the time is taken up focusing on areas that are clearly administrative, then not much is left for the strategic discussions that are after all the work of the board. Routine housekeeping-type board issues can be structured to take minimal time from the more important strategic discussions. Of course, this requires that the superintendent have the confidence to engage the board in the tough discussions over difficult issues.

Deep Learning

As trustees do their oversight, they need to pay attention to trends in learning, especially in times of transition. There are growing concerns that traditional schooling is less engaging for students and no longer relevant; in response, new approaches are being developed, such as deep learning. As discussed in Chapter 2 (Figure 2.1), these developments include the new global competencies such as the 6Cs: character, citizenship, collaboration, communication, creativity, and critical thinking (Quinn et al., 2019). Deep learning is "quality learning that sticks with students." It focuses on the 6Cs or similar global competencies. It transforms the learning relationship between and among students and teachers. It is occurring because of the "push" factor that regular schooling is boring and ill-fit for 21st century complexity, and the "pull' factor that attractive learning alternatives are being developed involving "engage the world change the world" scenarios (see Fullan, Quinn, & McEachen, 2018).

At times of innovation and transition it is crucial for trustees to be "in the know." It is not possible to fully develop a governance mindset without a commitment by trustees to do the deep thinking and learning necessary to make quality decisions. This includes how to consider and support innovations. But to decide on required changes, trustees must have confidence in the information provided by the superintendent and administrative staff. If trustees lose confidence in the quality or truthfulness of the information provided, it is virtually impossible to develop coherence. It creates a hole in the trust and confidence necessary to maintain a high-quality governance system.

Since trustees are dependent on the administration as their primary source of information on the district, it is incumbent on the superintendent to provide the high-quality data that make deep learning by trustees possible. If we want trustees to be evidence-based decision makers, then the superintendent has to provide evidence. If we want trustees to be quality decision makers, then the superintendent must provide quality information. If we want trustees to have a strategic focus, then the superintendent must provide strategic information.

To a person, the five superintendents we discussed earlier take this issue of providing accurate and authentic quality information to their boards as one of their highest priorities. They understand that if they expect the board to be part of the coherence in the district and to support the program internally as well as out in the community, they must have the best and highest quality information possible. Only then can deep learning really happen. Further, superintendents must help board members understand what is happening on the ground with respect to progress and strategies being employed. At the same time, they must be open to hearing board members' perspectives on what they are hearing from their constituents. It is better to be transparent (thereby dealing with both good and bad news) than to keep trustees in the dark. The latter almost always comes back to haunt you compared to dealing with issues head-on. In the end governance-minded superintendents see governance as a joint enterprise and thereby establish strong bonds of trust with their boards.

Manner

High-performing, purposeful superintendents understand that the best way to help everyone understand the importance of manner is to model the behavior and demeanor they expect from their trustees and staff. The pie chart presented in Chapter 2 (Figure 2.2) on trustee mindset and manner applies equally to superintendents. Everyone is watching the superintendent, but trustees even more so.

This is a sensitive area for superintendents. Most superintendents understand that it is not advisable for them to lecture their trustees on behavior. Therefore, purposeful superintendents understand the importance of approaching this issue by supporting the establishment of a governance infrastructure that includes adopted norms and protocols. Discussed more fully in Chapter 6, the ground rules reflected in norms in particular establish a standard of behavior for everyone on the governance team.

The Power of Joint Mindsets

We haven't done a cost analysis comparing superintendents who failed to develop the kind of mindsets we have been describing with those who have attended to these matters. We suspect that the reader is well ahead of us on this one. The short-, mid-, and long-term costs of lack of understanding of core governance principles as reflected in a lack of a governance mindset are enormous: conflict, mistrust, low performance, frustration, costly personnel cases, superintendent and other staff turnover, frequent instability, and much more. The governance mindset takes time at the front end, but represents a lasting bargain once established. Good mindset relationships keep on giving; bad ones keep on taking.

CONCLUDING COMMENTS

Much has been said and written about governance issues in education. Controversy exists over the tenure of superintendents and their relationships with governing boards. The key message from our work is that in fact there are vibrant examples of excellent long-term working relationships, where according to governance lore, there should not be. There are many complex, high-performing districts with low-income, at-risk students that have long-serving superintendents who have strong two-way relationships with their board. What is clear from our five examples is that there is a direct relationship between purposeful board superintendent engagement, a shared moral imperative, a collaborative, trust-based governance culture, and sustainable, long-term success. Were these superintendents just lucky to have good board members, or did they cultivate strong unified relationships with their boards? We would put our money on the latter. Yes, it takes hard work and constant reinforcement of positive relationships to make it work over time. The results for children, however, far outweigh the challenges to adults.

4

Welcoming New Trustees

· ·

I t is puzzling how any new trustee could be expected to be fully informed and high performing immediately after joining a board. In almost every organization, public and private, more attention is being given to "onboard" someone new by providing him or her with a full complement of tools, an explanation of the culture of the organization, and a clear definition of roles and responsibilities. There is a saying in governance circles that one new trustee creates an entirely new board. How newly elected or appointed trustees are brought on to the governance team will in many ways determine how that board will function from that point on. It is not possible to overemphasize the importance of welcoming and onboarding a new team member to the governance team, yet few organizations do it well.

When Onboarding a New Trustee

1. Begin afresh in addressing system-wide coherence and the district's moral imperative.

2. Introduce the new trustee to the board's governance culture.

3. Orient the new trustee regarding the concept of a governance mindset.

4. Reinforce the focus of the existing members.

Onboarding a new trustee is an opportunity to accomplish four very important things. First, it is an opportunity to begin afresh with new trustees in addressing system-wide coherence and the district's moral imperative. Second and perhaps equally important, it is a chance early on to introduce a new trustee to the board's governance culture. Third, orienting the new trustee as soon as possible around the core concepts of a governance mindset—systems thinking, strategic focus, deep learning, and managing your manner—will make a significant impact on the effectiveness of the new trustee. Fourth, it gives the board an opportunity to reinforce the focus of existing members.

The governance culture on a board is always subject to flux, and trustees with a governance mindset understand the importance of making a new trustee a valued member of the team. This is not as obvious or easy as it seems, since many elected trustees join a board with individual agendas, preconceived notions about the district and the board. In some cases, they may have run against and defeated a board incumbent who might have been friends with the remaining trustees. Or they may have campaigned against some of the current trustees and the board that they are now a part of. The need for new trustees to seamlessly become a part of a unified, well-functioning board requires a major commitment—especially from veteran trustees.

The issue of governance culture and new trustees can be complicated and complex. There are instances of negative governance cultures where addition of new trustees provides an opportunity for real improvement. Obviously, this can be difficult because of the constraints inherent in simply being new. Even in these cases, the wisest posture of new trustees is to listen, learn first, and then act as appropriate.

THE FIRST 100 DAYS: WHAT THE BOARD SHOULD DO

There are four key steps that a board can take to help new trustees feel welcome and a part of the board.

Help the New Trustee Feel Welcome

1. Set up a meeting with the superintendent and board chair. Find out about the goals, priorities, talents, and connections of the newcomer.

2. Individual board members should reach out with a note or a phone call.

3. Arrange school site visits and classroom walkthroughs to introduce the new trustee to faculty, staff, and students.

4. Arrange an in-depth discussion meeting with the full board. Give the new trustee the opportunity to comment on the shared core beliefs and values of the board, the moral imperative, and the strategic goals.

Meet With the New Trustee, Chair, and Superintendent

Set up a meeting with the superintendent and board chair as soon as possible after the new trustee is elected or sworn into office. This informal orientation session should serve two reciprocal purposes. One is to find out about the goals and priorities of the newcomer. It may turn out that the new person has goals that represent constituencies and issues that have not yet been adequately addressed by the board. Or it could be that the new trustee has talents and connections that would further serve existing goals.

One of the main purposes of the initial meeting is to provide the new trustee with the information necessary for understanding the complex organization of the school district. The superintendent and board chair should be prepared to answer any and all questions with candor and authenticity. However, it is important for both the chair and superintendent not to appear to be lecturing the new trustee or inferring an "our way or the highway" message. This is an opportunity to communicate the governance culture of the district. And as we have just seen, the first meeting is a two-way street to find out the reciprocal interests of newcomers and incumbents.

This session should not take the place of a private meeting between the superintendent and the new trustee. It is important for the superintendent and trustee to get to know each other and begin to establish a governance relationship.

Extend a Personal Sign of Welcome

This is a time for individual members of the board to reach out to the new trustee, with a warm welcome to the board. Sometimes a new person is unsure about joining an established board, particularly if the board has a long history together. A personal note, email, or phone call is a very welcoming gesture and signals an openness and receptivity on the part of the board. This is particularly important if a contested election created tension or outright hostility between individuals.

Arrange a School Site Visit

As soon as feasible, site visits should be arranged, which will allow the superintendent to introduce the new trustee to faculty and staff at the school level where the children are. It can be very invigorating for trustees to learn more directly about the work of principals and teachers by observing the instructional process in the classroom. For many, it is the beginning of an entirely new perspective.

Meet With the New Trustee and the Full Board

As soon as possible, the board should arrange an in-depth discussion meeting for the new trustee with the full board where all aspects of governance in the district can be explored. At this meeting, the new trustee should be given the opportunity to discuss and provide input into the shared core beliefs and values of the board, the moral imperative, and the strategic goals. Most important, this is when and where the members of the board can actively listen to the new trustee. Listening respectfully and empathetically may be the most important step a board can take to bring a new trustee into the positive governance culture of the board.

Just as in the case of the board chair and superintendent initial meeting, it is important that the board not use this time to "lecture" the new trustee or in any way attempt to pressure him or her into "falling in line." This is particularly true if there is a perception that a less than positive culture currently exists on the board. Every time a new trustee joins the board, it's a new board. The new trustee may in fact bring a breath of fresh air to the board culture.

> Every time a new trustee joins the board, it's a new board. The new trustee may in fact bring a breath of fresh air to the board culture.

This is where the governance handbook discussed in Chapter 8 is so helpful. The governance handbook or similar document should be reviewed and time spent with the full board discussing the protocols, the role and responsibilities, and the norms that the board has adopted as a framework for the board's governance culture. The value of this discussion is not just for the new trustees; it is also an opportunity for current trustees to revisit these same topics and recommit their support. At this time the superintendent can review major issues that the board is currently addressing and challenges in the future.

It should be made clear to new trustees that a unified board is not a lockstep, uniform board and that divergent opinions and points of view are welcomed and encouraged. Trustees should understand that they are part of an important team and that their point of view will be woven into the fabric of the district's governance culture.

Most important, the board should suspend all judgment about the new trustee regardless of how well known the person is, the nature of his or her campaign, or the person's past history. The new member was elected (or in some cases appointed) just like everyone else on the board. Preconceived notions and assumptions cannot be allowed to become self-fulfilling prophecies. Many new trustees are alienated because they believe they are prejudged and, as a result, not listened to. Because of this, these trustees often become the source of tension and stress throughout their board tenure. People often change depending on how they are approached. Treat them for the better, and chances are the board will reap the benefits.

THE FIRST 100 DAYS: WHAT NEW TRUSTEES SHOULD DO

1. Suspend all preconceived notions about the district, the staff, and the board.

2. Get up to speed in a reasonable amount of time.

3. Be mindful of confidentiality, the special nature of trusteeship, and relationships with organizations.

4. Avoid conflicting interests.

5. Accept the realities of governance.

6. Understand that time is your best friend.

The most important decisions a new trustee makes are the choices early in his or her tenure. Trustees choose whether to develop a governance mindset, to learn to be a systems thinker, or to pursue a strategic focus. They choose whether to invest the time and energy in being a deep learner. They choose whether to manage their own manner. Or not.

Many trustees, both appointed and elected, will often confess that being on the board was an entirely unexpected experience. No matter how many board meetings they observed from the audience, nothing could prepare them for the scope and complexity of board governance. Once on the board, they realized that often they had been seeing only half the story. They quickly learn that there are always many sides to every issue. That issues they used to ignore when sitting in the audience, they must now engage in and eventually vote on. The first few months, even for the most experienced and involved community leader, can be very intimidating.

Suspend Preconceived Notions

As a new trustee, one must suspend virtually all preconceived notions about the district, the staff, and the board. As much as possible, trustees should not let past experiences or past relationships, good or bad, prejudice their ability to develop a governance mindset. As part of that, they need to understand the necessity of rising above personal history and biases. What matters is the ability of the board to govern as a team, to achieve the goals and objectives that the board has set. One of the counter-intuitive realities about board service is that the more a trustee governs professionally, as part of a unified team, the more personal stature and authority the trustee gains. Individuals who see the board as a place to win personal battles or achieve personal victories often lose both.

Get Up to Speed

It is the responsibility of a new trustee to learn the basics in a reasonable amount of time. The best way to do this is to ask questions, questions, and more questions. Asking questions at a board meeting is not micromanaging. Take particular care to ask for clarification about acronyms. One of the more face-saving techniques for the reluctant trustees is to say: "For the benefit of the audience would you explain what xyz means?" Better yet, ask that the board take care to spell out acronyms at least once in a public discussion. The truth is that half the people nodding knowingly, both at the board table and in the audience, may not know what it means either.

There are numerous resources available for new trustees, many of which should be provided during the board orientation. What to look for are the district/board policies, which are policies adopted by the board that direct all aspects of the district operation. Special attention should be given to policies that address the operation of the governing board. In some districts this section of the district policies includes operating rules as well as some specific norms. A second set of resources available in many districts are norms, protocols, and meeting guidelines adopted by the board. We discuss norms and protocols in more detail in Chapter 6. Of course, the new trustee should be familiar with the board's moral imperative as well as specific strategic goals adopted by the board. New trustees should also receive a copy of the district's latest strategic plan. One of the most valuable resources is the governance handbook described in Chapter 8.

Be Mindful

There are three additional points that new trustees need to keep in mind: the importance of confidentiality, the special nature of trusteeship, and relationships with organizations. Nothing will destroy trust in a board more quickly than a breach of confidentiality. The problem is that most new trustees don't know what is confidential and what is not. A new trustee must, as soon as possible, learn what is considered confidential.

For example, virtually all personnel matters and legal actions are considered confidential. The ramifications, both legal and financial for the organization, can be severe if confidentiality is breached.

An early lesson for new trustees is realizing that they can never take off their board hat as long as they are on the board. In everyone's mind, a trustee will always be a trustee and as such be privy to special information and have the ability to exercise power in the school district. This reality creates a number of challenges for new trustees. First, it can create a false sense of adoration, or its opposite, the devil incarnated. People might think you are great or that you are just short of evil. Your words have impact. A casual comment at a cocktail party, at the grocery store, or even to close friends is taken seriously and can often contribute to confusion or may affect outcomes far beyond what the trustee ever intended with the comment. Second, when approached in any informal or formal venue, questions asked, some seemingly innocent, must be taken seriously. Gossip is not policy. As difficult as it may seem, trustees with a governance mindset learn to never say such things as "I will fix that for you," since as individual trustees they do not have the authority to do so.

Avoid Conflicting Interests

Another area to consider is the impact of trusteeship on your ability to continue with citizens' groups, particular advocacy groups, where special interests might overlap with your duty as a trustee. For example, as difficult as it may seem, parents who have often been active in local PTAs, school site councils, or advocacy groups who get elected to school boards must seriously consider whether they should continue to actively participate with those groups. In no way does this mean you cannot support such groups, but being seen as too closely tied to any single group, however noble, in the area in which you govern, could very easily create conflicts with the broader strategic agenda of the organization.

This gets to the issue of never being able to take off your board hat. When you participate in any activity in your school or community, you are always a board member, and everyone knows it. This often extends to family. There is an example of a board member whose daughter was sent to the school nurse because she was feeling bad. While checking her out, the nurse spent the time telling the board member's daughter about the cuts in the health supplies and the need for additional resources for the nursing staff in the district. Needless to say, the student only wanted to feel better and go home. Whether it's at the grocery store, the movie theater, a school site council meeting, the trustee is always on call.

Understand the Realities of Governance

Perhaps one of the most difficult challenges for new trustees is the realization that they do not, as individuals, have the authority to implement changes or "fixes" to major problems that motivated them to join the board in the first place. They quickly realize the three realities of governance:

The Three Realities of Governance

1. You are elected as an individual, but you must govern as a member of a team. You didn't get to pick the team; you may not even like everyone on the team, but it's your team.

2. You do not have authority as an individual trustee to fix the problems you promised to fix in your campaign. Only the board has authority to take action.

3. Your success as a trustee is completely dependent on the success of your board. The public, appropriately, tends to judge the success of the board by the board's accomplishments, not by what individuals do.

As discussed in Chapter 2, although many board members come to the board with ideas and goals related to a single agenda or special interest, new trustees soon learn the pitfalls that creates. They learn that it is difficult, perhaps impossible, to carry out the systemic governance responsibilities of the trustee if he or she is driven by only one interest or belief and does not make the transition to the full board strategic agenda. While it is important for trustees to be informed by their passion and beliefs, care must be taken not reach an extreme where compromise is difficult and maybe impossible.

Understand That Time Is Your Best Friend

Perhaps most important is to understand that time is the best friend of every new trustee. Being the board rookie has some real advantages. The smart trustee will use this time to soak up, like a sponge, as much information as possible. One of the realities is that the organization did not start the day a trustee was elected or appointed. Joining the board is like jumping on a train running at full throttle. It is not unreasonable for a trustee to take up to a full year to learn all the intricacies of the school district the board is governing. It is important for trustees to internalize that because they are serving multi-year terms, there is plenty of time; everything does not have to be done in the first year.

10 Important Additional Things for a New Trustee to Remember

1. Be patient. . . You were elected for a term of office; take advantage of the time to learn. You are only new once.

2. Choose to govern professionally; it will determine your legacy. Most important, develop a governance mindset.

3. Be a systems thinker. Connect the dots.

4. Have a strategic focus. Understand and be proud of the awesome responsibility of setting the direction for the district.

5. Commit to deep learning. Always do your homework. You cannot be part of something you don't understand.

6. Be trustworthy; build trust with your board, your district, and your community.

7. Contribute to creating a positive, powerful board culture; understand how your board works.

8. Represent the needs of all your community, not a part.

9. Be a leader on your board, in the district, in the community.

10. Always remember you and your board are modeling the ethical and moral standards you expect the children in your district to emulate.

CONCLUDING COMMENTS

Perhaps the most important way a board can sustain its positive governance culture and remain a unified, vibrant decision-making team is through the purposeful inclusion of new trustees. Change on boards is inevitable. If the board and superintendent take a well-thought-out approach to managing the onboarding of new trustees, viewing change as an opportunity to refuel and refresh the governance system can cause great things to happen. As we have seen in this chapter, the key is managing the process from start to finish, providing the new trustee or trustees with a welcoming environment, listening carefully and empathetically, and seeing change as positive. Positive governance culture is sustained and built upon by passing on the moral imperative and the norms to new generations of trustees.

> A board can sustain its positive governance culture and remain a unified, vibrant decision-making team through the purposeful inclusion of new trustees.

We have now addressed in Chapters 1 through 4 the critical foundational matter of governance mindsets. How you think individually, how you think in subgroups, and as a full group shapes how you are likely to act. Action brings with it new insights arising from how effective your behavior has been. Mindsets and efficacy are a two-way street. The former determine degrees of efficacy, and the latter operates as a feedback system for mindsets. Let's see how this works in the chapters of Part II.

Part II
....
Governing for Efficacy

5

Governing With Coherence

· ·

Enduring great organizations are characterized by a fundamental duality. On the one hand, they have a set of timeless core values and a core reason for being that remains constant over long periods of time. On the other hand, they have a relentless drive for change and progress.

—Jim Collins (2001, p. 35)

I n this chapter, we are going to dive more deeply into the conditions necessary to create a coherent, unified board around a shared moral imperative and unity of purpose. It is important to stress that we are talking about a unified board, not a uniform board. There is a big difference.

Uniform is defined by Merriam Webster "as having always the same form, manner, or degree; not varying or variable." When we think of uniform we tend to think of lockstep, everyone and everything the same. On the other hand, a unified board is made up of individuals, complete with different beliefs, styles, and personalities working together in a collaborative, cooperative fashion with a shared moral imperative toward a common goal. This is a very important distinction.

> A unified board is made up of individuals, complete with different beliefs, styles, and personalities working together with a shared moral imperative in a collaborative, cooperative fashion toward a common goal.

For trustees with a governance mindset, it all comes together when they find common ground from which to govern. They understand that sharing a unity of purpose is at the heart of board leadership. In order for school boards to be a part of system-wide coherence, they must first experience internal coherence within their own board. This turns out to be a very tall order, and to address this we need to add greater heft to our conceptual framework in relation to the process of *coherence making*.

COHERENCE

As we noted earlier, Fullan and Quinn (2016) published the book *Coherence* to help school systems focus and develop "a shared depth of understanding" that would guide their work. We based the book on our applied work with school districts in California, Ontario (Canada), and elsewhere. We said that coherence is elusive in complex systems and hard to maintain once you establish a degree of it. As usual with our work, we boiled the matter down to the smallest number of key, interactive components—in this case four (Figure 5.1).

We cautioned that the four components were not linear but were interactive and iterative. Focusing direction, for example, is key, but you can develop it effectively only through collaborative determination. Collaboration must be about the work, hence teaching and learning, including engaging pedagogy, is basic. Accountability is not something that can be tacked on at the end, nor can it be effectively front-end loaded. Rather, it is

Figure 5.1   **The Coherence Framework**

Source: Fullan & Quinn (2016)

infused in the process throughout, whereby a culture of internal account-ability linked to external performance measures is established.

School districts and others across North America and elsewhere saw our book *Coherence* as the route to salvation (until they found that it is not self-evident where to start and how to go about it). We continue to work on this matter, additionally publishing a tool book titled *The Taking Action Guide to Building Coherence in Schools, Districts, and Systems* (Fullan, Quinn, & Adam, 2017), that contains 33 protocols for action.

What we did not do in *Coherence* was to link, let alone integrate, dis-trict leadership and school board leadership. This is the task of the current chapter. We are encouraged by this possibility because two state school board associations have done a great job in stepping up and developing guidelines for their membership based on the *Coherence* framework (Iowa Association of School Boards, 2017; California School Boards Association [CSBA], 2017). The CSBA report summarizes their view on coherence:

> Research supports the importance of coherence to achieving a dis-trict's vision and goals for student achievement. Coherence does

not require that individual schools give up their autonomy. Instead, coherence provides guidance for how sites can be responsive to local conditions in a way that is consistent with school district priorities for achieving student gains. Boards can play a critical role in fostering coherent school district or county office of education actions and initiatives in order to stay focused on their essential goals and vision for student achievement. (CSBA, 2017)

They do show very clearly the relevance that the coherence framework has to governance and to trustees. However, these two otherwise very strong documents do not show governance as a *joint mindset* between trustees and superintendents in the way we conceive of it in this book. Shared depth of understanding *is* joint mindset.

Comparing What We Have to What We Need

Figures 5.2 and 5.3 compare the existing situation (Figure 5.2) to what we need (Figure 5.3). At best, current situations integrate management and instruction, thereby achieving a degree of coherence among educators, but not trustees. Our book is about Figure 5.3—overall

Figure 5.2   Current Coherence Mindset in the System

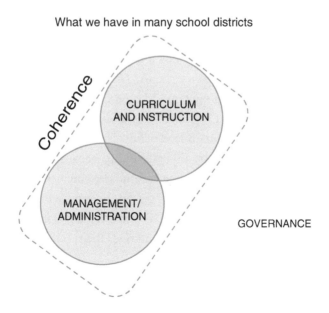

What we have in many school districts

Coherence

CURRICULUM AND INSTRUCTION

MANAGEMENT/ ADMINISTRATION

GOVERNANCE

Figure 5.3 **Required Coherence Mindset in the System**

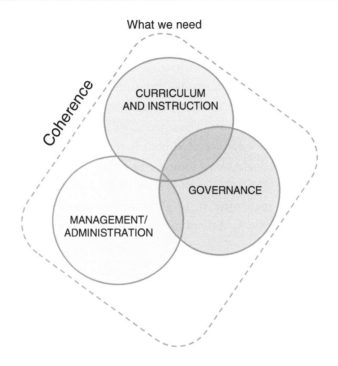

coherence between and among educators and trustees that integrates management, governance, and the education mission of the district and its schools.

It will not be sufficient for trustees to work on coherence as a group. Fundamental progress will depend on schools, boards, and superintendents to work on coherent governance *jointly*—this is the essence of the governance mindset.

Fundamental progress will depend on schools, boards, and superintendents to work *jointly*—this is the essence of the governance mindset.

COHERENCE MAKING

It is easy to say that a board should come together to agree on a deeply held moral purpose, but actually making it happen is a challenge and requires purposeful action. Notwithstanding the difficulty, reaching agreement on a commonly held moral imperative leading to the board's unity of purpose is the threshold for effective governance. The dominant characteristic of most dysfunctional governing boards is their inability to find common ground. They rarely if ever have unity of purpose. At the core of this lack of coherence is a lack of understanding and agreement about the nature and purpose of the work of the district.

It is here that we appreciate the interactive nature of the coherence framework. There are two foundational elements to developing a unified board: collaboration and trust. The importance of creating a collaborative culture on teams is widely accepted both in the literature and in practice. After all, when was the last time someone said they were opposed to collaboration? Unfortunately, however, this seems to fall into the category of often preached, seldom implemented; or perhaps implemented superficially—people can collaborate to do nothing or to do the wrong thing. What is required is that the organization develops highly specific collaboration related to the moral imperative they are pursuing. Thus, focusing direction (moral imperative and action therein) and collaborative culture are intimately related. They must happen in concert.

The following statement is at the heart of building coherence on the school board: "Collaborative work is a key driver in the shifting behavior. It is the social glue that moves the organization toward coherence" (Fullan & Quinn, 2016, p. 73). The goal is for collaboration to become "the way we do things here." Creating a collaborative culture doesn't just happen because it sounds good. There are a number of specific conditions and behaviors that must exist if such a culture is to develop. "Deep collaborative work requires new ways of working together, trust, shared leadership, sustained focus, and a commitment to collaborative inquiry" (Fullan & Quinn, 2016).

Of all the characteristics mentioned above as a requirement for creating a culture of collaboration, perhaps the most important on a school board is trust. Lack of trust makes collaboration virtually impossible. "Collaboration moves at the speed of trust," writes Chris Thompson (2015), who works with cities for the Fund for Our Economic Future. Additionally, Thomas Friedman (2016) writes:

When people trust each other, they can be much more adaptable and open to all forms of pluralism. When people trust each other, they can think long term. When there is trust in the room, people

are more inclined to collaborate and experiment–to open themselves up to others, to new ideas, and to novel approaches–and to
extending the Golden Rule. They also don't waste energy investi-
gating every mistake; they feel free to fail and try again, and fail
again and try again. (Friedman, 2016, p. 359)

Trust is an elusive concept. It is very difficult to get and very easy to
lose. It is particularly difficult on a school board composed of individuals
elected or appointed from the community that commonly have different
perspectives and, in many cases, substantially different political and social
orientations. Trustees may have campaigned against incumbents on the
board or the board itself and now find themselves attempting to build a
cohesive team with them. It takes real patience and understanding on the
part of the veterans as well as a suspension of assumptions by new trustees. Building trust in this environment requires hard work and effort. It
requires a commitment by all trustees to be open and willing to learn from
each other. You don't get trust by saying "Please trust me." Trust has to be
earned through action. You have to prove you are trustworthy in terms of
both reliability (I keep my word) and competence (I am skilled at follow-
through). Trust is more an outcome than a precondition, but once you have
a degree of it, it can become a powerful causal force, albeit and unfortunately, perilously easy to lose.

Trustees with a governance mindset have a unique understanding of the
importance of building trust. They will apply both their systems thinking
and strategic focus and, most important, their understanding of the impact
of manner as they work toward building trust with their colleagues. At a
National School Boards Association Conference, Glen Tecker observed
that trust is about respect and understanding, not agreement. That is an
important point. Most people begin to trust someone when they feel listened to, understood, and respected.

Here is a very simple example. A few years ago, in California, a prominent liberal Democratic legislator, John Vasconcellos, was authoring a
piece of legislation. He directed his staff to meet with a colleague of his
from across the aisle. Vasconcellos was among the most liberal Democrats
in the legislature, and the person he was directing the staff to meet with
was probably the most conservative Republican member. He almost never

voted with Vasconcellos. When asked why he wanted the staff to meet with him, Vasconcellos responded, "because I respect him, I understand his philosophy, and because of that, I trust him and know that what he says will be his position" (personal observation, ca. 1982).

Perhaps even more powerful is the statement from the late Senator John McCain, the distinguished and widely admired Republican leader, in his eulogy to Senator Edward Kennedy, the prominent Democratic leader:

> We disagreed on most issues, but I admired his passion for his convictions. He had an uncanny sense for when differences could be bridged and causes advanced by degrees. He was the best ally you could have. Once his word was given and a course of action decided he would honor the letter and spirit of the agreement. (2009)

Trust is when members of a board have faith that the motivation and inherent beliefs of colleagues on the team are honorable, ethical, and honest. It is quite possible, and indeed not uncommon, to have philosophical and political differences and still find common ground about the purpose and goals of the organization. Understanding and respect for differences in the context of shared organizational values build the foundation for trust. Perhaps the most famous leadership guru in the United States, Warren Bennis, writes the following:

> Trust is the lubrication that makes it possible for organizations to work. Trust implies accountability, predictability, and reliability. Trust is the glue that maintains organizational integrity. (2007)

COHERENCE IN PERSPECTIVE

The most important thing to remember about coherence is that it is fully and only *subjective*. As we said earlier, alignment is rational; coherence is emotional. If coherence doesn't exist in people's hearts and minds, it doesn't exist at all! Our standard is higher because organizational coherence requires *shared* understanding among large numbers of people. The latter requires continuous interaction to sort out meaning and arrive at deeper understanding. We decidedly do not mean that everyone agrees on everything, but rather that there is enough interaction and adult learning going on that some differences are resolved, new shared meanings are achieved, and remaining differences are understood. In this way the content of coherence gets continually refined.

We have also discovered that coherence is never a once-and-for-all state. Organizations must have the capacity for *continuous coherence making*. There are three reasons for this. One is that there are always people coming and going—newcomers arrive, others depart. Second, the environment changes: demographics shift, new policies are generated, and random occurrences both good and bad are visited upon us. Third, hopefully incumbents have new ideas that are intended to push the organization forward. In the final analysis, think that coherence is crucial, that it requires constant interaction, that "talking the walk" reflects its presence, and that when it comes to communication you should take nothing for granted. Interact, specify, test, reflect. Mindset is a multilane highway with many players. If you carry out this work well, you will be rewarded with greater impact and satisfaction.

DISTRACTIONS AND CHALLENGES TO COHERENCE

Creating a unified board around a unity of purpose is not an easy task. There are a number of challenges to that unity that must be addressed and resolved. Trustees with a governance mindset understand that these challenges can serve as serious obstacles to building trust and a collaborative culture.

Distractions to Coherence and Unity

1. Balancing individual core values and the board's unity of purpose
2. Micromanagement or accountability?
3. Representing a constituency
4. Having a single agenda/one program/one purpose
5. My way or the board's way: Is compromise selling out?

6. The rubber stamp conundrum

7. Confidentiality

8. Trustee leader or follower?

9. Handling trustee professional expertise

10. What do I do when I vote "no" and it passes?

1. Balancing Individual Core Values and the Board's Moral Purpose

Perhaps nothing is more challenging for trustees, particularly those newly elected, than knowing how to reconcile their core values and beliefs with the development of a shared moral imperative and board strategic goals. As emphasized earlier, the basis for creating a collaborative culture is finding ways to balance, as a board, the various individual beliefs and values of trustees. For many trustees, this can be a difficult task. While at no time should any member of the board violate their core base values in their work on the board, the issue is whether those beliefs guide the work of the trustee or provide a straitjacket that tightly constricts the ability of the trustee to govern as a member of a unified team.

As the board engages in discussion, the challenge becomes one of communication based on a foundation of trust and respect. If trustees find they cannot communicate with each other in a respectful and authentic manner, reaching agreement on something as fundamental as a moral imperative will be difficult. A strong, collaborative culture on the board is a necessary foundation for communication and will go a long way toward addressing perceived differences between values and core beliefs of trustees. For the individual trustee, a personal decision must be made whether a particular issue or disagreement is so basic and such a violation of his or her core values that he or she cannot reach agreement.

Where will the line be drawn on whether a particular issue violates a core belief? Trustees with a governance mindset are so clear about their internal moral compass that there are actually very few issues that do not provide an opportunity to develop an agreement without violating their core beliefs. While the ability to vote is a good way to force a decision when constructive discussion has ended, it is not a good way to deal with potential conflict around core values, particularly when the board is discussing the moral imperative. We recognize that current political conditions in the United States and elsewhere hamper and in many cases make coherent mutual development unlikely, but if there is one domain where common ground might be found, it is in education. In California, for example, where much of our work is based, there is a currently a strong common foundation on which to build. There are many other states where education could form a common rallying point for societal development.

2. Micromanagement or Accountability?

The dreaded M word: *Micromanagement*—the word that raises the hackles of trustees and superintendents, the concept that is most often misunderstood. What is one person's micromanagement is another's accountability. Micromanagement has been described, tongue in cheek, as when the board does something the superintendent does not like. It is difficult to precisely define because it has become a code word for perceived inappropriate trustee behavior. Micromanagement, as the name implies, is almost always an intrusion into the administrative or instruction roles—into how the district carries out the direction of the board. It also tends to be an issue with individual trustees, not the board. As such, it is important for both trustees and superintendents not to use the word loosely when referring to a board. Although it is difficult for boards to micromanage since the board can take action only by a vote of the majority in a public meeting, it does happen. However, most micromanagement occurs behind closed doors in one-to-one or small-group settings. If an individual trustee shows interest in a given issue on behalf of a constituent, it does not automatically mean that he or she is micromanaging. It is when they try to get favorable decisions behind closed doors that it becomes a problem. Otherwise, it is just doing their jobs to become better informed and to be concerned about those they represent.

Why do some trustees micromanage? Actually, many don't know they are doing it, thinking that what they are doing is what they are supposed to do. There are at least eight specific examples where micromanagement is likely to occur.

Examples of Where Micromanagement Is Likely to Occur

1. Some trustees confuse micromanagement with accountability. They don't understand the difference and are often convinced that reaching deeply into the organization is the best way to personally evaluate programs. It is extremely difficult to not make "suggestions" for improvement along the way, which may be interpreted by staff as interference. Often trustees don't understand that when they make a recommendation or even a mild suggestion in a one-on-one conversation with a staff member, the staff may take that as implicit or explicit direction. The influence of a member of the board in those situations cannot be overestimated.

2. Sometimes it occurs when trustees have lost confidence in the superintendent and/or the administration. This often is a result of fear—fear that the superintendent or his staff is not carrying out the direction of the board, or district leaders are not doing a good job in administering the district (Gottlieb, 2001).

3. Some trustees who come to the board with special professional or personal skills can't resist using those skills in a district setting. For example, attorneys, accountants, and human resource professionals often have a difficult time easing into those functions as they are carried out in the district.

4. Many trustees are used to fixing things and accomplishing tasks, not setting direction and establishing policy. It can be difficult to feel that you are sitting on the sidelines when major programs approved by the board are being implemented.

5. Governance does not create immediate rewards where administrative decisions and directions often show short-term results.

6. There are no norms or protocols adopted by the board that govern such behavior.

7. Trustees may want to demonstrate or exercise what they perceive is their authority, forgetting that they actually have no authority as an individual member of the board.

8. Trustees may try to intervene at the administrative level to solve a problem for constituents.

In reflecting upon this list, it is clear that micromanagement is usually a result of lack of structure, organization, and governance discipline on the board. Trustees with a governance mindset are clear about their focus; they rarely, if ever, micromanage. They understand that the governance job is systemic and strategic. Virtually no incremental intervention into administration comes close to that definition. In fact, no one is more distressed by individual micromanagement by their colleagues than trustees with a governance mindset. They understand that it is a major distraction from the cohesive work of the board.

Lecturing individual trustees is not the best way to deal with micromanagement. The best remedy lies in the board operating with a strong governance infrastructure framed by governance principles, norms, and protocols. Add to that a collaborative, trusting governance culture with open communication between the superintendent and board, and micromanagement disappears as a significant governance issue.

3. Representing a Constituency

Another challenge to the work of building a unified board arises when some trustees are conflicted about the balance between representing a constituency and supporting the strategic district agenda. It is not unusual for a trustee to feel pressure to be the "voice" of a particular group. Often this occurs because of support provided during an election campaign or identification with a specific group in the community. This issue is sometimes overstated, as no one should expect trustees to turn their backs on the people who helped elect them or appoint them. They might be friends, professional colleagues, advocates for special programs, or any number of different combinations.

As in most cases, the issue is balance. This matter goes to the heart of representation, equity, and the board's moral imperative and strategic goals. It is one thing to treasure a relationship and another to let that relationship undermine the system work of the trustee and board. Years ago, a brilliant education leader in the California Department of Education, Marion Joseph, was asked if there was a shift of power when authority was moved from the superintendent to the principal in implementing school site decision making. Joseph responded, "Wrong question." A very powerful statement: The right question was, "What is the responsibility of the superintendent and principal in implementing this program?"

In the context of constituencies, when a trustee is asked, "Who do you represent?" the response should be, "Wrong question." The right question is, "What do you represent? What is your internal moral compass and how does that guide you in your trustee role? If the district's moral imperative is reflected in the district's purpose and work, and if you are part of that purpose and are committed to system-wide coherence, that should be answer enough. Trustees with a governance mindset understands that deep learning prepares them to lead rather than respond to pressures from external yet sometimes friendly groups. Being able to justify positions taken with solid, well-reasoned explanations, equips the trustee to teach and educate, not just defend.

A difficult representation issue that can cause conflict arises when members of the board are elected from trustee areas rather than district-wide. Do trustees represent the trustee areas that elect them or the entire district? Again, wrong question—in this case a false dichotomy. Trustees cannot allow themselves to be forced into an artificial choice: trustee area versus the district—a few children versus all children.

Of course, trustees from a given local jurisdiction will have a special relationship with the area that elected them. However, a trustee with a governance mindset will be committed to achieving the moral purpose of the district even if that sometimes means disproportional allocation of resources. Issues like continuous improvement, equity, and quality instruction serve all children. The systems thinking, strategic focus, and deep learning of the governance mindset will guide the trustee in his or her relationship with his or her trustee area.

4. Having a Single Agenda/One Program/One Purpose

A question was asked at a trustee workshop: "How many of you, when you ran for office, said the following? 'When I get on the board, I promise to do absolutely nothing: I have no agenda, I have no axes to grind, no favorite program. Vote for me and I will bring no agenda to the board.'" Of course, almost no one raised her or his hand. It is a reality that the whole purpose of running for a school board is to bring something to the table. So, challenging that reality is not only a waste of time; it is counterproductive because it creates unnecessary conflict and generates a defensive reaction at the outset of a new trustee's tenure on the board.

It can be a problem, however, if a trustee is elected, has a single agenda focus, and never moves beyond it: It becomes a classic case of looking through a telephoto lens with no peripheral vision. Ironically, most of the issues that trustees address and on which they vote have nothing to do with the special program or agenda the trustee originally had when joining the board. The challenge for single-issue trustees is to be as committed to the core issues of the moral purpose and strategic goals of the board as they are to specific points in their agenda. Does this mean that trustees cannot have preferences, goals that they want to achieve for the district while on the board? Of course not. What it means is that trustees must balance their concerns and commitments with the overall strategic agenda of the board. They can be advocates for certain programs and issues but should not be locked into a position that narrows their vision or understanding of the broader issues and programs consistent with the board's strategic agenda. They have to be careful not to let their commitment to one issue or program shape how they view the overall agenda of the organization. As they develop a governance mindset, they will begin to put that early commitment to single programs or issues into proper perspective and only then will begin to govern the entire organization, bringing the same level of passion and commitment to all programs supported by the board.

5. My Way or the Board's Way: Is Compromise Selling Out?

One of the major challenges to trustees with a passionate belief in a program or issue is the concern that in the process of working with the board to develop a unified strategic agenda, they might be accused of selling out. Advocates for programs sometimes place significant pressure on a trustee not to compromise his or her beliefs and commitments just to reach agreement on a broader agenda. This creates a false narrative, assuming that somehow by working within the group to find common ground a person is sacrificing his or her core beliefs. Edmund Burke wrote, "All government—indeed, every human benefit and enjoyment, every virtue and every prudent act—is founded on compromise and barter."

This negative perception of compromise can be a serious obstacle to developing a unity of purpose on a board. Establishment of a positive governance culture based on deep learning, systems thinking, and strategic focus, reinforced with norms and protocols, will allow trustees to demonstrate how the strategic agenda of the district will fulfill the needs of all the children in the district. Hard data showing the improvement of the quality of education for children is the best rebuttal.

6. The Rubber Stamp Conundrum

For some trustees their greatest fear is being viewed by their community as being in the pocket of the superintendent and staff. They often will state with some pride, "I am not a rubber stamp for the administration." They are proud of their independence and view it as essential to carrying out of their trustee role. This is a case of confusion between the accountability role of the board and its stewardship function. By virtue of appointing the superintendent, in its stewardship role, school boards have a responsibility to ensure that the district has the support and resources to implement the strategic direction set by the board. If staff is carrying out the direction of the board, why would the board not support the staff? If, on the other hand, the board disagrees with the staff's recommendations or believes the staff is not carrying out its direction or does so in a less-than-competent fashion, then in its accountability role, the board must take corrective action with the superintendent. Once again, balance is the key. However, the board should never not support the district staff simply because they do not want to be viewed as being "staff driven" or being charged with not fulfilling its oversight responsibility.

This entire rubber stamp notion should be irrelevant. Every trustee should be engaged in the deep learning required to make informed governance decisions. By doing so, the board is fully prepared to make objective judgments and decisions about virtually every aspect within their scope of responsibilities. We have found in our coherence work that once people gain a shared depth of understanding about the work through purposeful interaction they will be able to "talk the walk" and therefore carry out their decision making in a confident and informed manner.

7. Confidentiality

Nothing will betray trust on a board more quickly than breaching confidentially. Many new trustees do not understand how significant this is. The problem with violating confidentiality is that it creates a hole in trust that is difficult to crawl out of. There are real consequences that trustees may or may not understand. These fall into three broad areas.

The first is related to district personnel. Every person in a school district has due process rights guaranteed by either state statute or by judicial case law. If a trustee violates confidentiality relative to a personnel issue, the board and district are liable for violation of due process, which is a very serious charge. Second, whenever a district is in any legal proceeding, all of its work is confidential. Any violation of confidentiality can have serious consequences for any potential court case or other legal proceedings. Third, work by the board in closed session is confidential by law. Only those items that are allowed may be discussed in closed sessions, and violating that confidentiality can have serious repercussions for the board. If a trustee is unsure whether something is confidential, it is a simple matter to ask for clarification from either the board or the district's legal counsel.

8. Trustee: Leader or Follower

Many trustees are elected or appointed because they are perceived to be good leaders. Once on the board, however, they are expected to be good followers as well—on the surface a real contradiction. With the exception of board officers, everyone elected to a board has the same power, the same job, and the same limitations as everyone else. For many, this creates a difficult problem and is challenging their sense of individual leadership. Leaders are wanted on the board, but the board cannot be led in five or seven different directions. Learning how to channel that leadership is a major challenge for trustees. The most successful boards learn to appreciate the intrinsic collective impact and power in people working together. One of the world's most successful medical institutions, the Mayo Clinic, describes itself as "Teamwork at Mayo Clinic: An experiment in cooperative individualism" (Clapesattle, 1941). Nothing says it better. "Cooperative individualism" is an excellent description of the balance between individual strength and leadership and the importance of teamwork. Fullan (2019) found in his book, *Nuance: Why Some Leaders Succeed and Others Fail,* effective leaders recognize that autonomy is not isolation. Autonomy and collaboration can feed on each other in a virtuous cycle.

> "Cooperative individualism" is an excellent description of the balance between individual strength and leadership and the importance of teamwork.

9. Handling Trustee Professional Expertise

One of the biggest challenges for trustees is the balance between personal professional expertise and the individual trustee role. At what point does the professional background of a trustee place that trustee in a superior position relative to his or her colleagues on the board? Is he or she truly better informed? The answer here is the same as elsewhere: it depends. Mindful trustees are very sensitive to the potential conflict between the individual expertise of a trustee and the professional needs of the organization they govern.

Examples abound. Is a trustee who is an attorney the final voice on legal matters affecting the agency he or she governs? Does the professional experience of the attorney trump the backgrounds and experience of other trustees when considering an issue with legal implications? This is a difficult question representing a serious balancing challenge for the trustee. As in many cases of governance, the answer lies in the gray areas that exist between the board and staff depending upon the size and scope of the organization. For example, in a very small school district with a very small staff, a trustee with legal experience might make a valuable contribution.

In larger districts, however, with more staff, the potential conflict between trustees' professional background and district staff or contract professional staff on any given issue is greater. In these cases, trustees must exercise great care in assuming that their professional background means their opinions carry more weight than those of their colleagues. Continuing the trustee/attorney example, the trustee with a governance mindset is informed by his or her legal experience but understands that he or she is not the organization's attorney and would not attempt to impose a legal opinion on the board. Rather, the trustee would help the board understand what questions might be raised and answered by an independent attorney formally advising the board and staff.

In another example at a governance workshop when addressing the issue of the role of professional expertise, a trustee raised his hand and asked, "I am the human resources director for my company. Was it wrong for me to ask to review all the job descriptions for positions in my district?" Yes, it was wrong. Unless the trustee was appointed to the board to serve as the organization's personnel director, the trustee who attempts to do staff work is in an untenable position. Who is going to hold that trustee accountable if he makes a mistake on those position descriptions? How can the board hold the individual trustee responsible since all the trustees are equal and do not have authority over each other? Certainly, the board cannot hold the superintendent responsible; after all, the superintendent works for the board. The answer is to not go there in the first place. Trustees' professional experience does not provide license to insert themselves into the operation of the district.

10. What Do I Do When I Vote "No" and It Passes?

Votes are not very good indicators of anything but an action in a snapshot of time. Voting outcomes are not necessarily an indication of unity. However, what a person does when he or she is on the losing end of a vote is a reflection of the degree of unity in the board. It is not necessary to have unanimous votes to have a unified board. A 5-0 vote doesn't mean it's unified, and a 3-2 vote doesn't mean it's not a unified board. In fact, vigorous open discussion often leads to split votes. But once a vote is taken, a unified board moves forward to the next issue, leaving behind any discord or hurt feelings. It is not uncommon for individuals to vote against each other and then be on the same side with the very next issue. It's about not taking things personally; it's about understanding that the importance of trust and respect allows boards to move on.

Often a question arises: What am I supposed to do when I vote no on an important issue, the issue passes, and then someone asked if I support the vote of the board? One answer, given by a very wise trustee, was this: "This district is governed by policy. The board as a whole makes policy. I am obligated to abide by the policy even if I voted against it. If I can't, then I will resign from the board, but I will not undermine the implementation of the policy. To do so would seriously damage the ability of the board to govern and the district to carry out its mission."

Boards with governance mindsets are reluctant to end a controversy by vote and would often spend more time on problem solving about the issue before bringing it to a vote. However, there is a time, even in the most heated debate and dialogue, that issues must be resolved and formal action taken. Boards that are unified are comfortable with split votes, and they have no residual impact on relationships or anything else. They simply move on to the next issue. The relationship that exists among trustees is stronger than any individual vote.

CONCLUDING COMMENTS

As we noted above, autonomy is not isolation. Prolonged isolation is bad for the individual and for the organization. However, being your own person while you collaborate can be a win-win proposition. People who are autonomous can have good ideas. When they are with the group, those ideas can make a contribution to the group; that individual can also learn from the group, thereby becoming better autonomously. It is a reciprocal relationship. Autonomous people can and should take their own stand on important issues, but that does not mean that they are not also team players. In our experience, disagreements can be valuable, and when there is two-way interaction, people tend to sort out their differences with the number of disagreements becoming smaller in number, and, in a sense, all the more important because they have been carefully considered. Coherence making as a process arrives at greater consensus while respecting remaining differences.

The moral imperative, unity of purpose, and coherence are the essential elements of effective governance. How they come together in sequence and the power and veracity of their existence determine the degree to which the board can carry out its governance responsibilities. What we know is that developing a governance mindset is a prerequisite to achieving the level of unity and coherence necessary to build a unified governance team. System-wide coherence without governance cannot exist. Building a unity of purpose based upon a shared moral imperative is not easy. Because governance is so complex, there are many challenges to building that unity. In this chapter we have identified the most common challenges and have provided suggestions about how boards might address them.

6

Governance Culture

· ·

Our Board serves as a model of the collaboration and mutual respect it encourages throughout our system. Our Governance Team believes in the concept of Team Mountain View, which is our shared belief in supporting all our students to be successful, meeting their diverse needs, and creating conditions in which all employees are valued and supported.

—Superintendent Lillian Maldonado French,
Mountain View School District, California (2018)

You can walk into a boardroom and within a few minutes determine whether this is a cohesive, high-performing board or not. Highly effective boards are characterized by an atmosphere of professionalism and trust. Trustees treat each other with respect and dignity and seem relaxed and easy with each other. Hard questions are offered both to the staff and fellow trustees with respect and professionalism. Debate is vigorous but not rancorous. Most important, the trustees address important, strategic questions and do not dwell on administrative issues. Split votes do not appear to be a problem and therefore do not cause concern. This collective behavior by the board is extended to their treatment of staff and community members. This is in stark contrast to the boards when relationships deteriorate. It is not an exaggeration to say that when boards disintegrate into dysfunction, the impact can be felt throughout the organization. Nothing undermines confidence in governance more than when adults exhibit behaviors in public that would never be condoned in private or even on a playground. The first lesson that each trustee should learn is that disruptive, unprofessional behavior is unacceptable.

> It is not an exaggeration to say that when boards disintegrate into dysfunction, the impact can be felt throughout the organization.

Perhaps the greatest challenge to internal board cohesion and a root cause of dysfunctional board governance is the culture within which the board operates. Governance culture refers to what is acceptable and expected in board operations and what is not. As Edgar Schein, one of the field's long-standing authorities on culture, puts it:

> As a group works together and faces common problems, it gradually builds common assumptions about itself and norms of conduct. In other words, the group as a group learns how to cope with its problems of external survival in its environment and to manage and integrate its internal processes. The sum total of this learning, embodied as a set of implicit assumptions that come to be taken for granted, can be thought of as the "culture" of that group. One of the main aspects of this culture will be the norms that guide group members' behavior. (Schein, 1999, p. 186)

Governance culture is the result of choices that individual trustees make about establishing norms and infrastructure (governance principles, protocols) in the board setting. Even more important, it's about whether trustees follow the norms they have established. Boards get to choose whether they will be effective or not—whether they will be a cohesive team working on behalf of the children or a group of individuals who get together for meetings. There is nothing more discouraging than to observe a board that is perceived to be ineffective only to find that most of the problem lies with individuals' inability to work together. Most disputes on boards are not the result of differences in point of view or even beliefs; these can be resolved, but they are the result of personality disputes or conflict. Often clashes are not addressed and continue until they reach the point that trustees just don't like each other. In every case, when these disputes get out of hand, effective governance is not possible, and the board's ability to govern grinds to a halt.

Trustees with a governance mindset never allow this to develop to the point that it cannot be resolved. They monitor both their own manner and the manner of their board and intervene early to head off problems before they become so toxic that they disrupt the ability of the board to govern.

Part of the problem can be traced to the very nature of board governance. Serving on a board is not a natural activity. On the one hand, when we serve on a board, we do so with the expectation that we will make a personal contribution and will provide leadership for change. On the other hand, we are told that we have no individual authority to take policy action on our own. Only the board can do the latter. Add to this the potential awkwardness of the different working styles of members, and we have a volatile mixture. Sometimes that mixture simmers until it boils.

Everything discussed to this point, governance mindset, cohesion, trust and collaboration, is dependent on the ability of the board to function together. The challenge is to bring a group of equal—elected or appointed—citizens together and expect them to govern as a unified cohesive team. We expect them to govern the most complex institution serving the children of their community in a reasoned, professional manner. It is an expectation that must be met if the district is to be successful.

PROCESSES THAT DEVELOP GOVERNANCE INFRASTRUCTURE

There are three important processes that assist boards in developing the governance infrastructure that is essential to fostering and sustaining a positive governance culture: (1) board-adopted governance principles, (2) norms, and (3) protocols. When the board is in the early stages of developing the governance structure, it is important to follow these processes sequentially. Governance principles are the most straightforward and, in some respects, the "safest." Having the group experience success in conversation begins to create the environment for more in-depth, potentially challenging discussions. The process is very straightforward. Once governance principles are established, it becomes clear that having some ground rules regarding how the board will conduct its business is very important.

> There are three important processes that assist boards in developing the governance infrastructure that is essential to fostering and sustaining a positive governance culture: (1) board-adopted governance principles, (2) norms, and (3) protocols.

Governance Principles

High-performing boards not only function with a shared moral purpose or imperative; they also govern with a set of principles that guide their work. These principles become a framework of governance standards against which the board can measure itself. They are also a way for the board to communicate the principles it has established for its own work with both the district staff and the community. They represent a commitment by the board to high-quality governance and transparency.

In a workshop trustees were asked to review effective governance characteristics listed by national organizations and to identify factors common to highly effective boards (see Appendix II). For example, after comparing the lists of effective governance practices, the governing board of District 23, Central Okanagan, British Columbia, Canada, identified six governance principles that would guide the governance work of the board. The principles were originally adopted in 2002 and revised and readopted in 2016.

Governance Principles of the District 23 Board

1. Stay focused on student achievement and student wellness.

2. Govern together as a team with a common focus and purpose.

3. Govern in a transparent, open, and accessible manner.

4. Govern in collaboration with the superintendent and staff.

5. Maintain a high standard of integrity.

6. Make high-quality policy decisions based upon evidence and data.

One of the main benefits of this exercise is in the discussion by the board. Two things become immediately evident. First, there is consensus among national experts in governance around the fundamental nonnegotiable characteristics of effective board governance. It does not matter what system or what organization, public or private, elected or appointed: The core elements are the same. Ignore these realities, and it is virtually impossible to have effective board governance. Second, asking the question *What would it look like if we were doing this?* leads to a powerful discussion that helps cement the concepts into the governance infrastructure of the district. Accordingly, school boards should adopt a given set of principles that they prominently display and periodically review.

Norms

The most effective way to create a positive governance culture is to take preemptive action to develop a normative structure that sets board standards for how trustees will interact and work together. This usually involves establishing norms. Norms are simply descriptions of how trustees treat each other and others. Norms are very important as guides for what is acceptable and unacceptable behavior and exist whether they are identified or not. When norms are not explicitly stated, they become the habits by which groups perpetuate behaviors, some of which can become toxic and very disruptive.

Jeffrey Sonnenfeld, the Senior Associate Dean of Executive Programs in the Yale University School of Management, conducted a major research study on corporate governance. He wrote the following:

> It's difficult to tease out the factors that make one group of people
> an effective team and another, equally talented group of people
> a dysfunctional one; well-functioning, successful teams usually
> have chemistry that can't be quantified. They seem to get into
> a virtuous cycle in which one good quality builds on another.
> Team members develop mutual respect; because they respect one
> another, they develop trust; because they trust one another, they

share difficult information; because they all have the same reasonably complete information, they can challenge one another's conclusions coherently; because a spirited give-and-take becomes the norm, they learn to adjust their own interpretations in response to intelligent questions. (2002)

Perhaps the importance of norms is best reflected in a simple question raised by an insightful school district trustee: "Is our board behavior a model for how the children in our district should behave now and in the future?"

There are many examples of norms adopted by school districts. We use only one here as an illustration of what a good set of norms looks like, developed by the North Monterey County Unified School District School District in California (2018). In that case, the board took the broad norms and applied them to how they would be implemented in a meeting format.

> Is our board behavior a model for how the children in our district should behave now and in the future?

North Monterey County Unified School District Governance Team Agreements (Norms and Protocols)

School Board Operating Norms

We respect and support one another.

We communicate openly.

We focus on the needs of the whole district.

We welcome input.

We're willing to take risks for children.

We listen with our hearts.

We take our responsibilities seriously, but not ourselves.

We don't surprise staff, nor do we expect to be surprised by staff. (NMCUSD, 2018, p. 18)

Meeting Guidelines

- We will keep our focus on the best interest of our students, working with parents, community and staff.

- We will stay focused on our goals and avoid getting sidetracked.

- We will work toward the future—based on current information.

- We will all remember that all people in the district are important and contribute to our children's well-being and education. We will never dismiss or devalue others.

- We will communicate openly, honestly, and professionally and we will respect each other and our differences.

- We will give helpful feedback directly and openly.

- When we have a difference of opinion, we will deliberate the facts of the situation and avoid personalities. We will address process—not personalities.

- All team members will offer their ideas and resources.

- We will keep our remarks brief and to the point.

- We will build upon the ideas of others, look for common ground, and paraphrase for understanding.

- We will be supportive of board decisions and the work of the district.

- Each member will take responsibility for the work of the team.

- Anyone can call a "time out" if s/he feels the need for a break.

- We will respect meeting times: start on time, return from breaks promptly, and avoid unnecessary interruptions. (NMCUSD, 2018, p. 29)

What is the most serious challenge to the effectiveness of norms? What we call approve, file, and forget. The challenge is not creating and adopting the norms themselves, but rather ensuring that adopted norms are honored in practice. It is easy to feel self-righteous in identifying norms, easy to adopt them (who would vote against being honest, listening, and just being a caring nice person?), but very challenging to actually live them, and to confront them when they are violated. Perhaps the least controversial action by a board is to approve norms, file them away in a board policy book or other governance document, and never see them again as the reality of the work of the board dominates the trustee's attention. However, for trustees with a governance mindset, norms become very much part of their board leadership. They recognize the incredible power of norms in practice to affect the board's governance culture. High-performing boards not only adopt norms but also keep them fresh and monitor them in practice. They become part of the culture, part of "the way we do things here."

Protocols

The third step in building an effective organizational governance infrastructure is the development and adoption of protocols. (See Appendix I for a Template for Creating Board Protocols.) While most boards adopt some type of board policy to be included in the policy manuals of the district, highly effective boards go further and adopt protocols. Board policies are requirements that govern the district. Protocols are operating rules that provide structure for the work of the board. They are very specific and apply to all aspects of trustee and board governance. Protocols are written agreements adopted by the board to define everything from meeting structure to relationships with the staff and community to the scope of the board's responsibilities.

Harvard University professor Richard Elmore (2007), writing in the *School Administrator* magazine, emphasizes the importance of protocols:

> Protocols provide a predictable structure to the work. They define roles and responsibilities in discussions, they provide group norms, and they keep the work focused in a productive way.

Developing and adopting protocols on an as-needed, ongoing basis can become an important part of the governance culture of the board. If done on a regular basis, it can be a normal part of the board's work. Although many boards adopt protocols at annual retreats, they become particularly powerful when they are a part of ongoing board operations. The key to successful protocols is that the board do more than just adopt them.

Effective boards follow them. In addition, since regularly scheduled board self-evaluations are important, routinely evaluating protocols in the self-evaluation process can be an important part of the governance process.

Often boards will have one- or two-day annual retreats, usually for the purpose of building board cohesion and addressing potential or real problems the board might be experiencing in carrying out its role and responsibilities. It is not uncommon for such meetings to be coordinated by a professional facilitator. One of the difficulties of such meetings is that once agreements are reached, particularly on governance issues, rarely are they written down in any way that will live beyond the retreat. As such, these agreements, while making the board feel better, often don't affect the operational work of the board. This is mostly because members either don't recall the agreement, remember it differently, or just don't take the agreement seriously: a classic case of "approve, file, and forget." Effective protocols are living documents. They are used, referred to, monitored, and updated periodically.

Once a board adopts and uses protocols, it is hard to imagine the board operating effectively without them. Without protocols, each trustee is on his or her own to decide how to handle a plethora of governance issues. The difference between board meetings where the board has adopted standing rules or protocols and those that have not, are startling. You can tell right away. Boards are operating with an orderly and accepted infrastructure; meetings are smooth and efficiently run; trustees are professional in their demeanor and respectful of each other; and staff and the community treat everyone with dignity and respect. Where no protocols exist, the governance culture is like the Wild West, never knowing where anyone is at any given time, where conflict defines the board and people are poorly treated. It is interesting to note that well-run, efficient boards get their work done in a timely fashion. In boards without structure, with no self-imposed discipline, meetings go on forever. Trustees might want to bring a cot because they are going to be there for a long time.

Four Main Reasons to Adopt Good Protocols

1. The discussion leading to the agreement

2. Resolving problems before they occur

3. Orientation for new trustees

4. Benchmarks against which board self-evaluation can occur

Note: See Appendix I for a Template for Creating Board Protocols.

1. The Discussion Leading to the Agreement

Often people will ask for samples of protocols when considering developing protocols. Boards should avoid adopting someone else's protocols without debate. One of the most valuable aspects of protocols is the process used to develop them. The more extensive and rich the discussion, the better the result, and the more likely the protocol will be followed. One frequent unanticipated result of the protocol discussion is that the issue that motivated the need for the protocol is resolved by the consensus of the board when approving it.

An example of one problem with sample language is the case of one district that agreed to develop protocols and asked for samples, so they would have an idea of what others had done. A specific and extensive list of samples was provided. The board looked at them, liked them, and simply adopted the entire list in one evening. The problem? There was no discussion of each protocol, and the chances of them being implemented by the board was nil.

There is not a right or wrong protocol. The key is that the protocol be the result of the board's work, their words, and their agreement on how to conduct business as a board. What matter are the discussion and the agreement that follow. The protocol is simply a record of the board's agreement and a guide for action.

One of the values of protocol development can be seen in a recent board meeting convened to consider protocols for the first time. In the discussion, it became immediately clear that there were many issues below the surface that needed to be discussed. This is basically a good board, functioning well, but with a number of elephants in the room. The very first protocol discussion led to a vibrant debate over meaning of words, misplaced assumptions, and different understanding of "facts" about how the board was operating. Everyone agreed that it was a long overdue discussion. In fact, the conversation was so rich and productive that the actual protocol was simply a matter of recording the agreement the board had reached.

2. Resolving Problems Before They Occur

Protocols do two things. They provide guidance to the entire board, and they prevent problems from happening. Micromanagement is a good example. If there is a clear definition of the roles of individual trustees and that role is clearly reinforced in a protocol, then micromanagement should never be a problem.

Where possible, boards should be careful developing protocols for problems that have already occurred. Protocols developed after the fact often become personal. Protocols should not be adopted to punish someone who has misbehaved in the minds of the majority of trustees.

3. Orientation for New Trustees

One of the most practical uses of protocols is to help new trustees understand how things are done on the board, what is acceptable, and what is not. Without protocols, new trustees are left to either guess what the board procedures are or get information from individual trustees, which can often be confusing and contradictory or just wrong. Ideally, when the board goes through a formal orientation process with a governance handbook, the new trustee will learn the unifying principles, the agreed-upon role of the board, the norms of the board, and the board protocols.

4. Benchmarks Against Which Board Self-Evaluation Can Occur

It is very important that protocols not fall into "the approve, file, and forget" trap. One way to ensure that protocols are current and viable is to include them in the board's self-evaluation. If trustees are asked to evaluate the extent to which protocols are being implemented, two things happen. First, the trustee's awareness of the protocol is raised, and second, the discussion of the results of the self-evaluation around specific protocols is extremely valuable.

Ideally, protocol development should become part of the governance culture of the board. Protocols should be reviewed on a regular basis and new ones adopted as needed. The process should be simple and straightforward. While boards often use outside facilitators to help with the process, once the board becomes comfortable with the process, using outside consultants may become unnecessary.

CONCLUDING COMMENTS

We have provided a lot of detail in this chapter in order to be clear about the nature and importance of principles, norms, and protocols. In practice, the process of developing these procedures for one's own board does not have to be complicated. Remember, the power is in the conversation. Engaging in serious discussion while developing these procedures will enrich the board in many ways, not the least of which is to develop the habit of productive collaboration. Get a sense of what other good boards are doing; review, formulate, and consider your own list and possibilities; discuss and adopt a set for your own board; and monitor and revise its use at least annually. Make the resulting agreements a living part of your culture.

It is virtually impossible to govern effectively without a well-constructed, agreed-upon governance infrastructure. Every successful organization operates with some form of "rules of the road."

So too do effective governing boards. In this chapter we have identified three essential elements that provide a framework within which governing boards can operate: governance principles, norms, and protocols. All three are essential to governing effectively as a team. Governance principles provide the basic philosophical frame within which the board agrees to operate. Effective boards agree on commitments that define the characteristics of their governance. Norms address how they will govern—what the standards are that will guide the collective work of the board. Protocols provide the guide rails within which the board will function. Without agreed upon processes, procedures, and protocols, it is virtually impossible for the board to function in a cohesive, consistent, and professional manner.

One of the most encouraging aspects related to the examples we use is that the vast majority of these cases represent low Socioeconomic Status Systems (SES). While it is good for all districts to establish the structures and cultures of good governance, it is essential for those districts that face the deepest challenges to develop strong governance cores. We do know that effective districts have coherent, strong, respectful relationships between trustees and superintendents.

7

The Governance Job
Systems Thinking and Strategic Action

∙∙∙∙∙∙∙∙∙∙∙∙∙∙∙∙∙∙∙∙∙∙∙∙∙∙∙∙∙∙

Our jobs are a lot like taking a shower—one wrong turn and you're in hot water.

—Anonymous Board Member

We have discussed high-functioning trustees with governance mindsets, superintendents committed to purposeful action supporting high-quality governance, a unified board with a shared moral purpose, and a well-developed governance structure. Now comes the heavy lifting. In this chapter we are going to look at where it all comes together in the meeting-to-meeting work of the board. How the board carries out its responsibilities is the ultimate test of the quality of its governance work.

It is important to stress that these are *organizational* responsibilities (or jobs) that only a governing board, operating as a unit, can do. They are at the heart of the Governance Core. They are the levers by which a board provides necessary systems and strategic leadership. And, when done well, they are powerful, strategic game changers.

Much of the focus of the discussion around board responsibilities is around what boards ought *not* to do. Usually the discussion is around a vague concept that boards set policy. Period. End of discussion. In fact, much of the literature refers to ideal boards as "policy boards." What is missing is what constitutes policy. Is it a narrow definition, as many superintendents would believe, designed to keep boards out of administration? Or is it a broad, wide-ranging description of how policy is operationalized by boards? The problem with a limited definition of policy is that it tends to ignore the ongoing meeting-to-meeting work of the board. In most states, the board's jobs in public education are defined by state statutes, and in the case of nonprofit public schools, organizational bylaws. Most school boards are required to approve the district's budget, approve plans for curriculum and instruction and facilities, and approve the collective bargaining contract where applicable. Boards are expected to provide oversight and accountability. The list goes on.

We have centered the governance responsibilities of the Board on five core foci.

Governance Responsibilities of the Board

1. Establishing strategic directions and related outcomes

2. Providing ongoing policy direction and approval

3. Stewardship and support for the work of the district

4. Oversight and accountability

5. Community leadership

A clear definition and shared understanding of these governance roles and responsibilities are central to the Governance Core and critical to the long-term success of the district. It is not enough to simply support coherence making and to agree on the shared moral imperative. The board realizes the power of its role only when applying these to its specific responsibilities.

Figure 7.1 **The Governance Core: Board Responsibilities**

The importance of recognizing the interdependence and connectivity of the board's governance responsibilities cannot be overestimated. They are part of a reinforcing loop. Boards that align their responsibilities around the core moral imperative and strategic goals make a major contribution to focusing the work of the district and fulfilling their governance responsibilities. By doing this, the governing board will reinforce the system-wide coherence of the district and demonstrate the powerful role governance can play in continuous improvement for children. When the board's direction is clear and unambiguous and delivered in a unified manner, the board's positive impact is felt throughout the district (see Figure 7.1).

SETTING STRATEGIC DIRECTION

Of all the board's governance responsibilities, the most important and powerful is formally setting the strategic direction for the school district. Throughout our book we have emphasized the essential strategic and systems role for governing boards. It is in setting and *sustaining* the direction of the school district that the efficacy of this role is realized. Setting direction can be defined as moving from a conceptual understanding of the moral imperative to a well-developed, transparent, and highly focused set of policies and strategic goals. If the moral imperative is the heart of governance, then setting direction is its brain. Decisions made by the board here will have a profound impact on the success of the district.

The foundation for the long-range direction of the district rests with a series of strategic actions taken by the board. These actions include development and adoption of a shared moral imperative, and, based upon the moral imperative, priorities and strategic goals and success indicators. All should be developed in a collaborative culture with the superintendent, staff, and teachers and with the involvement of a broad range of parents and the community. The process is also iterative; each element feeds back in a continuous loop.

Setting direction: Moving from a conceptual understanding of the moral imperative to a well-developed, transparent, and highly focused set of policies and strategic goals

A note about organizational visions: Many years ago, a superintendent was quoted as saying, "Ten years ago if I had a vision, I would have been locked up; now I can't get a job without one!" As we said earlier, visions have had a poor track record for at least the last three decades. Indeed, for many, visions have become routine exercises, top heavy on aspirations but silent on how to get there. Organizational visions are a description of the end game: what the destination of the educational voyage looks like. There is danger in confusing beliefs with visions. Wanting to close the achievement gap is a belief; having closed the achievement gap is a vision. Shoulds and wants are not visions, nor are they strategies. Too many boards state their beliefs and stop there, as if their beliefs represent a direction. That is a mistake.

It is important to understand that setting direction is not a single event, nor is the journey to achieving the moral imperative a straight line. It is an ongoing, almost organic function of governance. In a healthy and productive governance culture, the superintendent and board, together, are almost always adjusting as they move toward achieving the moral imperative. When new trustees join, they are often challenged by the fact that the district is already on a strategic path, and while they may offer new perspectives, the district did not start the day they were elected or appointed.

It is also important for the board to understand that it is not sufficient to simply build a strong governance infrastructure with a moral imperative, governance principles, norms, and protocols. Trustees must always remember that the products of board work are not the structure and processes, no matter how sound. Rather the products are the increased quality of programs and greater outcomes for all students. All the strategic planning, community engagement, and professional dialogue mean little if the board does not take action by adopting well-developed, easily understood, measurable strategic goals and success indicators designed to achieve the moral imperative.

Once goals and indicators are adopted, it's the board's job to stay focused on strategic goals.

Timothy Waters and Robert Marzano (2006) in a working paper for Mid-Continent Research for Education and Learning (McREL) capture the essence of the board's responsibility for maintaining a relentless focus on the strategic goals of the district:

> In districts with higher levels of student achievement, the local board of education is aligned with and supportive of the non-negotiable goals for achievement and instruction. The board ensures that these goals remain the top priorities in the district and that no other initiatives detract attention or resources from accomplishing these goals. Although other initiatives might be undertaken, none can detract attention or resources from these two primary goals. Indeed, publicly adopting broad five-year goals for achievement and instruction and consistently supporting these goals, both publicly and privately, are examples of board-level actions that we found to be positively correlated with student achievement.

Part of the challenge for the board is to maintain its critical, long-term focus while also comprehending the rapidly changing dynamic world we live in. Setting direction is about charting a course into the future that will equip children with the skills and knowledge not only to succeed, but also to excel to the best of their abilities. It is in charting this course that systems thinking, strategic focus, and deep learning are essential.

> All the strategic planning, community engagement, and professional dialogue mean little if the board does not take action by adopting well-developed, easily understood, measurable strategic goals, and success indicators designed to achieve the moral imperative.

At the same time in an era of rapid change, we know that setting direction and being willing to adjust according to the dynamics of rapid change are essential. Ray Kurzweil, Director of Engineering at Google, and Chris Meyer write this regarding the rate of change:

> Part of the challenge for the board is to maintain its critical, long-term focus while also comprehending the rapidly changing dynamic world we live in.

We're entering an age of acceleration. The models underlying society at every level, which are largely based on the linear model of change, are going to have to be redefined. Because of the explosive power of exponential growth, the 21st century will be equivalent to 20,000 years of progress at today's rate of progress; organizations have to be able to redefine themselves at a faster and faster pace. (Kurzweil & Meyer, 2003)

Tom Goodman, senior vice president of strategy and innovation at Havas Media writes this:

> Uber, the world's largest taxi company, owns no vehicles. Facebook, the world's most popular media owner, creates no content. Alibaba, the most valuable retailer, has no inventory. And Airbnb the world's largest accommodation provider, owns no real estate. (Goodman, 2014)

The point is that change is happening around us so rapidly that we often can't even see it. A board's ability to chart a direction for the future depends on both maintaining what is working and addressing new challenges. As the late John Nicoll, a long-time superintendent of Newport Mesa School District in California, stated in his *So You Want to Be a Superintendent?* (1995) book of letters to his son:

> Your future success as a superintendent of schools will depend on how well you can adapt to societal change. The worth of the educational process to the children you serve will, in large part, be dictated by the way in which you and your board can change ˙our system to meet the demands that society will place upon your ˙dents. (Nicoll, p. 5)

As we have argued throughout this book, school boards and superintendents must become key partners in the direction-setting process. In our discussion of negative and positive governance drivers, we identified as a negative driver "simply informing boards" and "engaging boards" as a positive one. We also emphasized the importance of boards owning the issues rather than simply being audience members. Setting direction is a powerful example of where boards must be engaged in the process and own the results. Only then can long-term implementation be sustained over time. As we have seen in our chapter on superintendent governance mindset (Chapter 3), highly successful, purposeful superintendents find substantive ways to engage their boards early in the strategic development process, getting their input and direction and developing ownership so that by the time of the official adoption there are no surprises.

POLICY DIRECTION AND APPROVAL

Perhaps the biggest challenge to the systems and strategic focus of many boards occurs in the regularly scheduled board meetings. Nearly every board meeting includes action items requiring board approval. This is where much of the tension between administration and governance can occur. It is only natural that the gray area between the "what" and the "how," which expands and retracts from issue to issue, would be a natural flash point. This is where the trustee governance mindset is essential. Having a well-developed systems perspective and a strategic focus combined with a firm shared commitment to the moral imperative and strategic goals keeps the board grounded and focused. As the board considers important policy issues, it is essential that the board resist the temptation to dive into the administrative details that will distract them from their strategic role.

The governance framework discussed in Chapter 6—principles, norms, and protocols that frame the board deliberation—will often determine the quality of the board decision-making process. It is another reason why the investment by the board and superintendent in honest, authentic dialogue to create a collaborative and trustful relationship will help immeasurably as they move forward in carrying out their responsibilities.

The board's ongoing strategic policy direction can be clustered into two main areas: the board's fiduciary responsibility and adopting program plans and frameworks. Each area provides an opportunity for the board to carry out its strategic responsibilities and represents leverage for keeping the district focused on achieving the moral imperative and strategic goals.

Fiduciary Responsibility

The school board is responsible for the financial health of the district. The board is ultimately accountable, both to the state and the community for the school district's financial solvency. Thus, the overall fiscal plan and the budget, as a reflection of the plan, is a crucial component of the board's responsibility. During times of extreme financial difficulty and frequent shortfalls in funding, resource allocation decisions can be extremely challenging. It is important to understand that if there is a financial crisis in a district, no matter the extenuating circumstances, it is the board that is held responsible.

The district's budget is in reality a policy document equal to, if not more important than, the district's strategic plan. It is the budget that drives resource decisions that profoundly affect the actual implementation of district priorities and strategic goals. Various plans and goals on paper mean little if resources are not allocated to accomplish them. Recently a district chief budget officer stated succinctly, "If it's not in the budget, it's not going to happen."

It is here that the importance of the governance mindset becomes once again clear. Systems thinking, strategic focus, and deep learning are essential if the board is going to make sound financial decisions. The board's responsibility to approve budget priorities, adopt a budget, and track implementation plans provides an opportunity to exercise systems review by helping keep the district focused on the strategic agenda.

Adopting Program Plans and Frameworks

Much of the work of the board in meetings is to approve frameworks, programs, and plans necessary to the work of the district. Not all frameworks adopted by the board are equal. Focus becomes paramount. This is an example of where the board should spend time and energy on actions that directly support the strategic goals. For example, adoption of the district's curriculum framework and instructional program is the most direct way the board can engage issues in depth around the moral imperative. Continuous improvement, equity, closing the achievement gap, system-wide change, and coherence are all reflected in the instructional plans developed by the superintendent and staff and adopted by the board.

The board will consider a wide variety of other plans, agreements, contracts, and frameworks during the school year. Examples include

- Approval of the human resource frameworks

- Adoption of the collective bargaining agreement

- Approval of the district's facilities plan

- Approval of the district's home-to-school transportation plan

- Approval of the district's food services plan

The challenge for the board from a systems perspective is how and in what ways these programs support the district priorities and strategic goals. This requires deep learning in action. The board must stay current, vigilant, and up to date on the progress toward the strategic goals so that they can ask the important questions. To what extent does the district's facilities plan support the strategic goals? How does the district's food services framework support instruction and equity? What about home-to-school transportation and student safety? System-wide coherence is just that: system wide. It's about connecting the dots; this is systems thinking at work.

STEWARDSHIP AND SUPPORT

One of the least understood and most underappreciated jobs of any board is providing support to the district it is governing. Since the board shares the moral imperative and adopts the strategic goals of the district, approves the plans and policies that govern the district, should not the board also support the superintendent and staff in carrying out the board's mandates? The board's stewardship responsibility requires that the board use its considerable power and authority in ways that directly reinforce the work of the district. Principal among these is the responsibility to create and support a positive organizational culture in the district.

Examples of Steps the Board Should Take

- Act with professional demeanor that models the board-adopted norms and protocols

- Make decisions and provide resources that support board-adopted priorities and goals

- Stand by decisions made by the board

- Uphold board-approved district policies

- Ensure a positive personnel climate exists

- Celebrate board progress in student learning, while identifying lack of progress as an area of concern and action

Throughout this book, we have emphasized the importance of board manner and a positive governance climate. The demeanor of the board has a powerful impact, both positive and negative, on the morale of the staff and their ability to carry out the board's direction. It is the ultimate measure of support to the staff when the board governs by the principles it sets, establishes clear, unambiguous direction, and lives by the norms it has established. To do otherwise seriously endangers the integrity and quality of the education program of the district.

One of the most important ways a board supports the district is to make sure there are sufficient resources available to accomplish the strategic goals. Recall the statement made earlier that the budget is a crucial powerful policy document for the district. Systems thinkers understand that the decisions the board makes on the budget have a profound effect on the ability of the staff to accomplish the strategic goals. Systems thinkers connect the fiduciary dots. Governance is often about difficult resource decisions. Priorities and focus must guide those decisions.

There is almost always a political dimension to governance decisions. Trustees might deny it, but it is true. In many ways, policy is fundamentally about allocating resources and personnel. For example, understand that decisions about closing schools (almost always resource based) are always highly emotional; however, often so are decisions regarding the football coach (personnel based). They both can become political very quickly. (By political, we mean, in part, that passions can run very high on both sides of an issue and boards will feel pressured to take certain actions.) It is very important to the superintendent and staff that the board stand behind any decisions despite the politics. Nothing can be more discouraging than having a board reverse itself because a board decision caused significant pushback from segments of the community. If a decision turns out to be a mistake in that it did not accomplish what it set out to do, then it is understandable the decision would be reviewed. However, when the decision is simply disliked and/or the result of disagreement but the decision was sound, it is important for the board to support the staff in its implementation. This is a perfect example of the importance of shifting from the politics of campaigning to responsibility of governing as we discussed in the introduction.

The board has a profound impact on the district culture. The actions of the board, both explicit and implicit, communicate to the staff and community the organizational values of the district. In our discussion of positive and negative governance drivers (Introduction) we mentioned a proactive, forward-thinking culture as a positive driver. By proactive we mean: *Does the board support a culture that encourages new ideas and forward-looking programs? Or is this a district that is committed to defending the status quo and resistant to change? Does the board look for heroes or villains? Is the board quick to blame or to praise? Or does it display a stewardship and support stance that furthers the core work of the district?*

OVERSIGHT AND ACCOUNTABILITY

The governance job is not completed by setting the direction, adopting policies, establishing the structure of the district, and providing support. In addition, accountability is a crucial part of governance and essential to continuous improvement in the district. The board needs to know if the programs are effective. Are the plans working? What progress are we making in achieving our strategic goals? We are not talking about punitive accountability (a wrong driver) but rather accountability to strengthen the instructional program through district-wide coherence and continuous improvement. Richard Elmore (2004) made a key observation when he said, "No amount of external accountability will be effective in the absence of internal accountability." Internal accountability occurs when the board and superintendent together ensure that individual and collective responsibility is built into the culture of the district.

Because board oversight is dependent upon quality information, one of the most potentially damaging hot spots in the board relationship with the superintendent is the quality of the information provided. It is not possible to evaluate programs without solid, accurate data. Boards are completely dependent upon the quality of the data submitted by the staff. Assuming that trustees have done the deep learning necessary to understand the context of programs they have approved, they should be in a position to evaluate the quality of the information provided. If lack of confidence in the efficacy of the information develops, it can be extremely damaging to the relationship between the board and staff.

Another important accountability mechanism is the review of the effectiveness of policies adopted by the board. All too often, policies fall into the "adopt, file, and forget trap" discussed earlier in our book. Priority should be given to the policies enacted to support the strategic goals. Emphasis should also be placed on policies in place addressing children's health and security as well as the fiduciary responsibility of the board.

No discussion of governance accountability would be complete without addressing superintendent evaluation. Throughout this book we have emphasized the importance of the superintendent board relationship. Part of that relationship is having a healthy, positive evaluation system agreed to by both the superintendent and the board. Evaluations should not be viewed as punitive but rather as a way of cementing the relationship. It is important that the evaluation be focused mostly on achieving the strategic goals established by the board. The key message here is that there should never be surprises in the evaluation. Boards and superintendents should discuss progress throughout the year. Any issues or concerns should be addressed as they occur. Most state open meeting laws allow superintendent evaluations in closed sessions. Many boards schedule quarterly evaluation discussions. Boards should not wait if they perceive there is a problem.

COMMUNITY LEADERSHIP THROUGHOUT

We said before that the board and superintendent must not only work together but also have rapport with community needs—this is at the heart of the moral imperative that should drive policy and action. Part of this task involves fulfilling their responsibility to educate and lead in their communities. Once they become a part of coherence making in the district, highly effective trustees understand that a major part of their job is to educate and inform the community regarding the work of the district. They must be able to "talk the walk," that is, be clear and consistent about the main goals and related progress within the district (Fullan, 2019). This is not a responsibility that can be delegated to staff. While staff can be helpful by providing expertise, it is not staff's primary responsibility to go out into community forums and educate the public. That is the job of the superintendent and board. The community's support for the district will, in large part, be determined by the confidence expressed by individual trustees.

The ultimate test of success is what happens in the classroom, but the public's understanding will be enhanced by open, authentic communication from the board. A trustee's capacity to educate the community is in large part determined by individual commitment to deep learning. The extent to which they can talk the walk depends upon their deep understanding of the work and purpose of the district. It is neither helpful nor useful if trustees cannot provide in-depth data and information on the state of the strategic priorities of the district. Trustees, even as systems thinkers, cannot be expected to be experts on every aspect of the complex education system of the school district, but they can be expected to have deep knowledge of the three to five strategic goals.

It is crucial that when the board does educate the public, it does so with a unified voice. Engaging with the public is not the time for trustees to demonstrate conflict or disagreements that might exist on the board. If the public sees a unified board demonstrating a district-wide coherence around clearly stated, key educational goals, they will support the district.

But it works both ways. As Paul Richman, former Executive Director of the California Parent Teacher Association, stated,

> There is an important educate-and-lead component to community leadership, but also a critical listen, learn and facilitate inclusion part. Increasingly, boards must deepen their understanding about their role in helping make sure all groups within a school community have ways to provide input, are heard, and are represented—and making sure the district is proactive in seeking out these many, diverse voices. Understanding how to solicit, listen to, and process that input is also a vital part of a trustee's deep learning. (personal communication, 2018)

CONCLUDING COMMENTS

The governance job is complex, essential, and yet possible to define in terms of its main components. Governance is more than a responsibility; it's a job complete with specific tasks that only a governing board can do. But how they carry out their responsibilities is key to effective governance. A unified, committed, and purposeful governance system will create several powerful outcomes: It will link the moral imperative to the district's strategic goals, which the board must approve; bring a strategic focus to the board to exercise its authority; fulfill its fiduciary and programmatic responsibilities; provide support to the district on an ongoing basis; hold the district accountable with a continuous learning focus; and reach out to the community to build a strong base of support for the educational program.

While this chapter describes the main area of responsibility, there is yet another support system for effective core governance. This system consists of the "tools" and related support systems that assist effective decision making and oversight. This is the subject of Chapter 8.

8

Governance Tools

· ·

Special processes and strategies used effectively in many districts to support effective governance have proven very useful to school boards and superintendents. If we take the generic concept of tools—devices for implementing given ideas or things—there are tools throughout this book. We need to remind the reader about the critical importance of having a core framework such as the Coherence model we presented in Chapter 5. Tools are only as good as the mindset using them (or as we used to say, "A fool with a tool is still a fool"). Tools help you focus. They provide guidance in dealing with complex issues. They are not "things" to be implemented but rather are catalysts for changing the culture that you have in mind.

A great example of governance tools in action is provided by Babs Kavanaugh, a highly respected governance expert with an extensive professional practice. She describes her work with Mountain View School District in California, where she was hired to organize and structure the board's governance practices into a governance handbook. Kavanaugh makes the following observations:

> The end product of 3+ years of work with this district is a commitment by the entire governance team to thoughtful, purposeful governance.

> What are the ingredients that allowed this to happen?

> 1. The board members have a deep commitment to their community, many having attended the Mountain View schools as students themselves.
> 2. They recognize and value one another's perspectives and are willing to listen carefully, to adjust as needed, and to "move on" together following disagreements.
> 3. They believe in their superintendent and greatly value her commitment to data and transparency.
> 4. The board has deep appreciation for working collaboratively with the superintendent to address the challenges and celebrate district successes together.

> What are the conditions that sustain this work?

> - Significantly, the superintendent contract includes quarterly governance workshops, sometimes referred to as discussion meetings. These workshops provide a vehicle for the governance team to engage in reflective dialogue, where they can openly and nonjudgmentally consider the complex issues that are facing their schools, their families, and their community.
> - The *MVSD Governance Handbook* is a resource for the board and referred to regularly as needed or when a practice is in question.
> - Onboarding of new governance team members begins right after the election or appointment and continues for months, providing all members an opportunity to develop together into a cohesive team. Through its governance handbook, the team conveys its mission of educating all students as an irrevocable trust.

- The governance self-assessment tool is customized to the district, specifically assessing each of the governance protocols outlined in the handbook. The governance team annually reviews, updates, and completes a signature page approving their governance handbook.

As stated in the *MVSD Governance Handbook:*

> Public education is vital to the health of communities. School board members are responsible for ensuring that a school district's public education system is serving the needs of all students by providing equitable access to a high-quality education. (personal communication, 2018)

In this chapter we discuss four different specific tools as part of the Governance Core. Although most often used in a sequential way, each building on the other, any of the four can be used independently.

Governance Tools

1. Discussion meetings

2. Governance handbooks

3. Board self-evaluation

4. Board continuing education

DISCUSSION MEETINGS

A number of years ago, at a workshop, a newly elected trustee asked, "When do we get to just talk as a board? It seems to me that we never get to really discuss things together, we are so agenda driven." There was a shaking of heads, affirmations from other trustees in the room, both veteran and rookie. This was similar to another trustee observation, "Our problem is that we never get to relax and just talk through an issue. We don't have conversations that allow us to really learn where each of us in coming from." This is a frustration that is felt in boardrooms across the country. Due to open meeting laws (this is not criticism, but a reality), boards rarely have an opportunity to have informal, candid discussions with each other as a team.

This becomes a significant issue when thinking about how to build a cohesive, unified board so essential to effective governance. How can a board be expected to build a governance team if members cannot talk openly together, sharing ideas and visions? How can the board table be safe for different and conflicting ideas when meeting in a glass house with so many people watching, some with very large rocks? Under almost all open meeting laws, boards are expected to meet in highly structured, agenda-driven meetings, possibly the most difficult environment for open and candid discussion. The only exception is for specified, narrow topics in a highly regulated closed session. In many states with more restrictive laws, boards may only discuss items that are specifically spelled out in the board agenda. This creates a difficult obstacle for trustees to talk to each other informally as a board.

Highly effective boards find alternatives without undermining the spirit or the letter of the open meeting laws. One of these is the use of discussion meetings. These are formal, noticed meetings, usually with the superintendent and maybe one or two senior staff, to discuss general governance issues, reviewing or writing governance protocols, checking on how the meetings are going, or assessing the overall health of the board. It's also an opportunity for the superintendent to share strategic ideas about the future direction of the programs authorized by the board or to float ideas for board reaction to new approaches and ideas.

Although it is required that the meeting be fully noticed and held in public, when the meetings are about governance, board meeting attendees in the audience tend to lose interest fairly quickly. For example, in a major urban district in Southern California, a board that had been controversial for its dealing with contentious issues, scheduled a discussion meeting to step back and just have a conversation. After each trustee had an opportunity to share his or her overall view, the board began to focus on the positive steps about which its members could agree. At the end of the discussion, at a time for public input (yes, opportunities for public input are still required) a regular board watcher went to the podium and stated that she had been going to board meetings for years and this was the first time she had really had a chance to see the high level of commitment each trustee had for children. This commitment in the past had been lost in the noise of the board meetings. The board had lost sight of the fact that regardless of its positions on issues, board members in fact shared a common, what we would call now, moral imperative about children.

There are ground rules for effective discussion meetings. They are not agenda-driven business meetings. Nor are they study sessions with or without staff making major presentations or even retreats. Discussion meetings are an opportunity for boards to develop a shared understanding and reinforcement of positive governance procedures and processes. The goal is for discussion meetings to become part of the culture of the board—taking time, not in some artificial retreat setting, or in a formal board meeting, but taking time out in the regular course of the year, to discuss governance issues. These meetings are for building shared understanding and agreement. No official votes are taken. This is important for respecting the spirit of open meeting laws. Voting should be done in more formal settings with appropriate public notice regarding the specific proposed action. Confusing official action with the purposes of open discussion will undermine the whole purpose of a discussion meeting.

There are a number of positive by-products of discussion meetings. The comfort level established within the board during these meetings can spill over to the regular board meeting. Creating an environment where open and candid discussion of issues and beliefs are encouraged can lead to an enhancement of board decision making. But most important, discussion meetings allow trustees and the superintendent to take the time to develop the shared understanding that leads to the board's active participation and ownership of the moral imperative and district-wide coherence.

> Discussion meetings allow trustees and the superintendent to take the time to develop the shared understanding that leads to the board's active participation and ownership of the moral imperative and district-wide coherence.

GOVERNANCE HANDBOOKS

Most boards have some type of annual retreat. A consultant is brought in, meetings are facilitated, discussions happen, issues are addressed, and problems seem to be resolved. The only problem is that after a couple of weeks, things almost always seem to revert back to the way they were before the retreat. Why? Because most of the time, agreements reached by the board are celebrated but usually not recorded in a way that can be ingrained in the culture. Notes, minutes, or reports of the retreat without any way to codify specific agreements or actions have little lasting impact.

Retreats can create a false sense of accomplishment when everything is based on a feeling of goodwill. Unfortunately, in a school board, the half-life of goodwill can be disappointingly short.

The answer is simple. When action is agreed to, write it down. When the board and superintendent agree on something, there needs to be a mechanism to record the agreements that will not get lost in the fog of governance. The best way to do this is to develop a governance hand-book. Then agreements, whether transcribed into norms or protocols, have a place to live, a place where the board has access on a regular basis. For example, governance consultants (acknowledged in our book) and others in the California School Boards Association developed such a governance handbook that is currently being used by hundreds of districts statewide.

Once developed, the governance handbook is an invaluable tool. It should be a living document, growing as needed to reflect the changing conditions as the board moves forward. It is the ultimate test of transparency. It is important that the document be designed for accessibility. This means it must be readable, authentic, and plain spoken. Acronyms should be avoided. Education jargon should be minimal. This is where the core essence of the governance team can be found and made available to staff, faculty, parents, or anyone interested in the work of the board.

Perhaps the most valuable use of the governance handbook is to support new trustees. In this document, the rules of the road will be found, the norms that define what is acceptable and what is not and the protocols that provide the framework within which the board governs. When used as a discussion guide, it is invaluable for helping new trustees become acclimatized to the culture of the board. It is also valuable because it represents the board voice, not the voice of an individual, avoiding the feeling by new trustees that they are being lectured or managed by a particular trustee.

Parts to a Governance Handbook

1. A description of the board's moral imperative and unity of purpose

2. A description of the board and superintendent's roles and responsibilities

3. A description of the district's governance culture

4. The list of protocols adopted by the board

5. Board-adopted strategic goals

There are usually five parts to a governance handbook. First is a section that records the board's moral imperative unity of purpose. This is where the board's guiding philosophy can be found, its theory of governance and its governance principles. Put most simply, what does the board stand for? Most districts have a vision and mission statement, but the intent here is to go deeper and reflect the core moral imperative that drives the governance system in the district.

The second section focuses on the board's roles, responsibilities, and its jobs. This is an important section because many people, staff and community, don't know what boards do, what their job is. The governance handbook will include the strategic goals adopted by the board as part of its setting direction responsibility.

The third section addresses the governance culture of the district. It is here that the board's governance principles and norms are spelled out. The board's commitment to core values of communication, transparency, and ethical standards are not only reminders to trustees but also inform the community. The stress and strain of governance, the normal actions of individuals grappling with complex problems in public, often project an image of the board that is misleading. By communicating the norms of the board and most importantly following them, the board demonstrates its commitment to open and quality deliberation.

The fourth and fifth sections of the governance handbook list the protocols and strategic goals adopted by the board. Having the protocols in the governance handbook is a convenient and accessible place where they can be consulted as needed. The big issue, as stated previously, is the danger that protocols will be adopted and then forgotten. Part of that occurs when the protocols disappear after adoption never to be seen again. Placing the protocols in the governance handbook ensures that they are accessible and thus current and alive.

> Placing the protocols in the governance handbook ensures that they are accessible and thus current and alive.

BOARD SELF-EVALUATIONS

One of the major characteristics of effective governance is the extent to which governing boards conduct regular self-assessments of their own effectiveness. Often, the best judge of what works in governance and what needs improvement are the members of the governance team themselves. As part of an ongoing commitment to continuous improvement, board self-evaluation needs to be used as a conscious governance tool.

"If you can't measure it, you can't improve it" is a statement attributed to Peter Drucker. The most important effect of board self-evaluation as part of the governance culture is that it institutionalizes the assessment process. The message it sends is that the board is not above accountability. If the staff is expected to meet standards, then so must the board. It also is important that the self-evaluation is not punitive in nature. It should always be geared to improvement.

One of the latest findings about assessment is that it is most effective when built into the culture of feedback and self and collective responsibility. Fullan (2019) calls this "culture-based accountability" that was a core characteristic of the 10 successful cases that he studied.

> It is very important that the self-evaluation process and instrument be authentic and directly applicable to the board undertaking the assessment.

It is very important that the self-evaluation process and instrument be authentic and directly applicable to the board undertaking the assessment. Boilerplate, premade assessment instruments are useful as a model but should not be adopted in totality. One way to localize the evaluation is to make sure that each protocol adopted by the board is evaluated. Protocols will remain visible if they are evaluated. And perhaps the most valuable of all is the discussion of low-scoring protocols during the analysis of the evaluation results. This type of discussion will remind trustees why the protocol was adopted in the first place and will highlight any difficulties with its implementation.

CONTINUING BOARD EDUCATION

There are two instances when boards tend to seek the assistance from outside consultants: (1) when things are not working or are in crisis or (2) to strengthen their governance system. While seeking external help can be helpful to forestall a total breakdown in governance, when in crisis, it is difficult to treat the underlying effects that caused the crisis in the first place. It's like going to the governance emergency room when you need to treat an injury; fixing the cause is a longer-term project.

Boards have also been known to seek outside assistance to strengthen their governance system. These boards are committed to excellence both in the district and in governance. They see continuing education as a form of professional development for the board that is as important as professional development for the faculty and staff. There are numerous opportunities for boards to receive this kind of continuing education. The best and most reliable are from their professional associations, particularly state school board associations and their national counterpart, the National Schools Board Association. Many of these have specialized academies, new trustee institutes, and subject matter training. The state administrator organizations as well as the national association may also offer assistance.

It is a mistake to undervalue the educational opportunities provided by these resources. One of the major advantages is that the various workshops and conferences offer a chance for the board and superintendent to attend and learn together. The challenge of deep learning is which critical part of such key elements in the governance mindset should motivate trustees to take advantage of every opportunity to increase their understanding and skills in governance. It is interesting that every other aspect of public education has professional development built into the organization but is not always thought of for trustees and their boards.

CONCLUDING COMMENTS

Get your tool shed in order. Keep an eye on the fundamental issues: moral imperative, strategic focus, deep learning, and mind your manner. Use tools to help organize and focus on these systemic matters. Mutual coherence about the nature and daily pursuit of your mandate is what you are seeking.

At the outset, it is important to understand that it's the discussion by the trustees on the board that is most valuable, not the products or the tools themselves. The process begins with discussion meetings that provide the trustees and superintendent an opportunity to just talk or share ideas or concerns before they become problems. Discussion meetings should become part of the governance culture of the board. Increasingly, boards are utilizing governance manuals or handbooks to record the agreements reached in discussion meetings that spell out the basic framework of the boards' commitments and work. If boards do not record their agreements, the agreements do not exist.

The third tool, board self-evaluation, is an essential part of a governance infrastructure. If we assume accountability for everyone else in a school district, why not the board? One thing that is often neglected is assessing the effectiveness of board-adopted protocols. Every self-evaluation should include an evaluation of how well the board is adhering to the protocols it agreed to follow.

The fourth tool refers to the board's continuing education. Professional development is an accepted necessity for supporting growth and development with the administration and instructional functions; why not with governance?

When all is said and done, mindsets and tools go together to improve the culture and the performance of the district.

Part III

....

The Challenges Ahead

9

Rising to the Occasion

· ·

The nature of current schooling has passed its due date. Various studies show that as much as two-thirds of students and teachers find schooling boring or otherwise alienating. Inequity is dramatically on the rise with non-school factors of poverty, racism, health, welfare, shelter, and safety contributing to the miasma of problems facing schools. The future of the economy, unpredictability and scarcity of jobs, and the unknown role of technology add other uncertainties. Local and global conflict threatens basic conditions of social cohesion and stress.

Politics have become weird, and new transitions abound. Two of the regions in which we work (California and Ontario) are both in the midst of political change: As of 2019, California had a new governor and a new state superintendent, both elected positions. It is expected that there will be policy direction continuity, but many issues remain to be worked out in pursuing its equity and excellence direction. In Ontario, after 15 years of provincial government by the Liberals, the right wing Conservative Party was elected with an unspecified but radical agenda of tightening the purse strings and pursuing ad hoc policies (in Canada the federal government has no jurisdiction over education; each province and territory is autonomous with respect to education). Almost a year into a four-year term, Ontario was being led by what we referred to earlier as partisan politics with little shift to "governing for the whole population." Time will tell, but we see little of the governance mindset that we write about in this book. At this point in 2019, Ontario was and is about politics, not governance.

In times of turmoil it is crucial that local governments become stronger. We do believe that they need to become better partners upward in the system, but we also hold to be true that they need to have a degree of independence when it comes to interpreting state policy directions. Our fundamental premise remains the same: effective school boards and superintendents are *system players*. This means that local boards need to take into account state policies but must also interpret them in light of local priorities. Never has this role been so critical as it is now and will be for this century. Local and state politics represent a dynamic and not necessarily a simple hierarchical relationship. This makes trustee-superintendent joint mindsets all the more crucial.

To conclude, we offer a set of tips for each of the trustees and superintendents.

Tips for Trustees

1. You are in this for the long haul; it's a marathon, not a sprint.

2. Stay strategic and focused. Never forget: the bottom line is the children, not adults. Don't get distracted by administrative issues that you are not responsible for and pay other people to deal with.

3. Develop the mindset that will allow you to excel in every aspect of the governance job. Remember, governance is a system job and a strategic job and requires deep learning and managing your manner.

4. Never forget that governance is a team sport. The board is a team; you may not like the team; you may have even campaigned against some of the team, but it's your team now, and it wins or loses for children as a team. If the board succeeds, you succeed; if the board fails, you fail.

5. Work hard to develop a shared moral imperative that will define the work of your board and superintendent. This is the core upon which the educational program will be developed.

6. Work for system-wide coherence both within the board and with the board and the district. Everyone on the same page with the same understanding of the work and the strategic goals of the district ensures success for children. This is the golden key to success.

7. Your superintendent is the most important partner of the board and is crucial to the success of the education program. Develop a professional and respectful relationship and nourish it.

8. Be the model of civic leadership for your district's children. Don't disappoint them.

9. Don't expect credit. In high-performing successful districts, boards stay in the background, proud of their achievements but wanting the teachers and staff to get the credit. Being in the newspaper is usually not a good thing for boards.

10. If going to the board meeting is your most unpleasant experience, you are not doing it right.

Tips for Superintendents

1. Teach, coach, lead—but don't lecture. Provide the board with engagement opportunities. Every question is a learning opportunity.

2. Count understanding—not votes. Votes are deceiving. Votes get you short-term support, but understanding gets you long-term support and sustainability.

3. Forget about control. Control rarely works anywhere anymore but certainly not in governance. If you worry about control, you don't get the true nature of governance.

4. Coherence making is the secret to effective governance. Once that is part of the governance culture, everything else falls into place.

5. Make the board winners; create value for them. Help make the board experience valuable. Engage the board; show them the impact of the district's programs on children in real time. Make sure they own the successes and share in the failures.

6. Respect the governance function. How many have used the phrase *care and feeding of the board*? How many have used the phrase *care and feeding of the senior staff*? Not ever.

7. Depersonalize governance—operate at 1,000 feet. Do not get drawn into the drama.

8. Support the board's community outreach and leadership.

9. Watch your manner. Stay cool at all times; remember everyone is watching you.

10. If you hate or resent governance, maybe being a CEO is not for you.

ALL RISE

One of the good things about the paucity of attempts to improve local governance is that there is not a track record of failure and defeat. Yes, fragmentation and individualism have taken their toll, and some bad habits have been established through inertia. But the good news is that with new ideas and a degree of continuous turnover that is endemic to local school boards, there is an opportunity to turn around the nature of local governance over the coming decade.

On the one hand, we have a long way to go to improve local governance. Paul Richman (2018), the former Executive Director of the California Parent Teachers Association, put it this way:

> Until now, governance research and thinking hasn't evolved all that much. It has mostly centered on the board's role and been pushed along chiefly by "negative drivers" instead of "positive drivers." If we, as communities, state, and as a nation, are going to

advance the critical mission of public education, we must rethink and reinvigorate our approach to governance and focus on the positive drivers. There is a moral imperative to do so. (personal communication, 2018)

Without the framework we have provided schools, boards will be at sea. The governance core requires that trustees and superintendents jointly develop their future where *moral imperative* undergirds the educational foundation, and *coherence* is the frame. Within this powerful and dynamic duo, systems thinking, strategic focus, deep learning, and manner supply the daily fuel.

School boards are faced with ever more complex decisions with increasingly severe consequences if they get them wrong. Take technology, curriculum programs, or assessment systems, for example. Without a proper framework, the board is faced with a series of ad hoc decisions where millions and millions of dollars are at stake, not to mention the squandered opportunity to implement the moral imperative of raising the bar and closing the gap for all their students. See Fullan and Edwards (2017) for what it takes to integrate technology, change culture, and dramatically increase student achievement for all.

How could it be any different if trustees and superintendents lack a mutual coherent system of the kind that we have offered in this book? In the absence of such a system, all they have left is to fall back on disorganized personal opinions of individuals that are vulnerable to one shiny object after another.

The rise of local governance would be great and timely movement for what we called in Chapter 1 "leadership from the middle." At the very time that public education is being challenged to be the best it can be, the opportunities (and challenges) abound. There are greater concerns about inequity, worries that nationalized standards and testing are not the answer, and concerns that technology may be contributing to greater human isolation. There is also recognition that peer learning among and between students and teachers may be the best route and recognition that traditional schooling misses the mark and that deep learning holds great promise for a transformed system. In short, the time has come for local governance and system improvement to join together. For that, we need trustees and superintendents to join together to act inwardly and outwardly as system players.

We are, in other words, entering a crossroads point in public education. Certainly, the world is awry with unpredictable dangers and golden opportunities to rise to unimaginable heights in the history of humanity. Public education is arguably the centerpiece of success or failure. It will require a *system change* of radical proportions to rise to the occasion. Local capacity is no longer only an issue of local matters. The core governance role has evolved from protecting local democracy to becoming a vital force for changing the system itself. Our book is intended to inspire and show how trustees and superintendents, together, can strengthen local schools as they help make society at large become globally prosperous.

There is something uplifting to turn one's attention to a neglected but revered phenomenon such as local democracy in increasingly calamitous times. Now we can have the more powerful focus that we have developed in this book. It is time to refine the politics, champion good daily governance, integrate local and state priorities, and lead the creation of a new culture and system of deep improvement.

School board members and district superintendents, it is time to raise your game dramatically—something that can only be accomplished jointly. The education world needs you—indeed, society needs a strong local governance mindset in action.

Appendix I

Template for Creating Board Protocols

As part of the governance culture, protocols should be reviewed on a regular basis and new ones adopted as needed. The process should be simple and straightforward. While boards often use outside facilitators to help with the process, once the board becomes comfortable with the process, using outside consultants may become unnecessary. The following is an example of a simple five-step protocol development process taken from an actual board-adopted protocol.

Step 1: Identify the protocol to be developed and name it. In most cases, simply naming the need or issue is sufficient. For example, assume there has been some misunderstanding about how and when individual trustees can request information from the staff. The topic of the protocol might be an individual trustee's request to staff.

Step 2: Discuss and agree upon the reason the issue should be addressed. This discussion should lead to a short rationale for the protocol. It is important to agree on the issue the protocol is intended to address, and why it is important. At this stage it is often helpful to define the parameters for the protocol: any rules or regulations that must be followed, beliefs or values that must be honored, pitfalls that should be avoided, and so forth. Often the rationale begins with "we believe" statements like those in the following example for this protocol:

Rationale: We believe that

It is important for the board to make informed decisions.

In order to respond to requests for information and be informed in policy deliberations, it is important for individual trustees to be knowledgeable and up to date on major issues.

Quality information helps the board move forward.

It is important that individual trustee requests not burden staff.

Staff should be honest in assessing the impact of trustee requests on staff workload and resources.

Step 3: Discuss and agree upon the actual language of the protocol to be adopted by the board. Writing a protocol's specific language in a way that the board can agree upon is extremely important. For example, for this protocol, the language below defines what is acceptable trustee behavior:

Individual Trustee's Request to Staff

Individual trustee requests directly to staff for information should be restricted to those requests that do not require allocation of staff time or district resources to develop a response.

Any trustee request that requires other than incidental staff time or any district resources to respond shall be referred to the full board for discussion and action.

Individual trustee requests for information should be directed to _____.

Step 4: Adoption of the Protocol. If at all possible, protocols ought not be adopted with split votes if more than one trustee disagrees since the entire board is expected to operate within the protocol scope.

Step 5: Once there is an agreement on a set of protocols, governance teams should determine when and how protocols will be monitored, evaluated, and reviewed. For example, the governance team may agree to review all protocols annually at a governance workshop or whenever a new trustee joins the team.

Appendix II

Three Comparisons of Effective Governance Principles

Twelve Principles of Governance That Power Exceptional Boards (BoardSource)	The Group of Thirty on Effective Governance (Effective Corporate Governance Practices)	Eight Characteristics of an Effective School Board (National School Boards Association, Alexandria, VA)
1. Constructive partnership	1. Fashion a leadership structure that allows the board to work effectively and collaboratively as a team, unified in support of the enterprise.	1. Effective school boards commit to a vision of high expectations for student achievement.
2. Mission driven	2. Build, over time, a nuanced and broad understanding of all matters concerning the strategy, risk appetite, and conduct of the firm.	2. Effective school boards have strong shared beliefs and values about what is possible for students and their ability to learn.
3. Strategic thinking	3. Take a long-term view on strategy and performance, focusing on sustainable success.	3. Effective school boards are accountability driven, spending less time on operational issues and more time focused on policies to improve student achievement.
4. Culture of inquiry	4. Respect the distinction between the board's responsibilities for direction setting, oversight, and control, and management's responsibilities to run the business.	4. Effective school boards have a collaborative relationship with staff and the community.
5. Independent-mindedness		
6. Ethos of transparency		

7. Compliance with integrity	5. Reach agreement with management on a strategy and champion management once decisions have been made.	5. Effective boards are data savvy.
8. Sustaining resources	6. Challenge management, vigorously and thoughtfully discussing all strategic proposals, key risk policies, and major operational issues.	6. Effective school boards align and sustain resources to meet district goals.
9. Results oriented	7. Ensure that rigorous and robust processes are in place to monitor organizational compliance with the agreed strategy, risk appetite, and all applicable laws and regulations.	7. Effective school boards lead as a united team with the superintendent.
10. Intentional board practices	8. Assess the board's own effectiveness regularly, occasionally with the assistance of external advisers. (The Group of Thirty, 2012, *Toward Effective Governance of Financial Institutions*, Washington, DC)	8. Effective school boards take part in team development and training. (National School Boards Association, 2000, *Key Work of School Boards*, Alexandria, VA)
11. Continuous learning		
12. Revitalization (BoardSource, 2005, Washington, DC)		

References

Authier, P. (2018, October 16). Legault tells his CAQ caucus to stay humble, represent all Quebecers. *Montreal Gazette*. p. A3. Retrieved from https:// montrealgazette.com/news/quebec/74-caq-mnas-to-be-sworn-into -office-as-party-slowly-takes-control

Bennis, W., & Nanus, B. (1985). *Leaders: Strategies for taking charge.* New York, NY: Harper and Row.

Bennis, W. G., & Nanus, B. (2007). *Leaders, second edition: Strategies for taking charge.* New York, NY: HarperBusiness.

BoardSource. (2005). *The source: Twelve principles of governance that power exceptional boards.* Washington, DC: BoardSource.

Brickell, H. N., & Regina H. P. (1988). *Time for curriculum: How school board members should think about curriculum, what school board members should do about curriculum.* Washington, DC: National School Boards Association.

California School Boards Association. (2017). *The school board role in creating conditions for student achievement.* Sacramento, CA: California School Boards Association.

Carver, J., & Carver, M. (2009). *The policy governance model and the role of the board member: A Carver policy governance guide.* San Francisco, CA: Jossey-Bass.

Clapesattle H. (1941). *The doctors Mayo.* Minneapolis, MN: University of Minnesota Press.

Collins, J. (2001). *Good to great: Why some companies make the leap and others don't.* New York, NY: Harper Collins.

Collins, J. (2005). *Good to great and the social sectors.* Boulder, CO: Monograph.

Covey, S. (2017). *The 7 habits of highly effective people: Powerful lessons in personal change.* Miami, FL: Mango.

Danzberger, J. P., Kirst, M., & Usdan, M. (1992). *Governing public schools: New times, new requirements.* Washington, DC: Institute of Educational Leadership.

DiMarco, M. (1989). CSBA president's column. *California Schools Magazine.* Dec.-Jan., 1989–90.

Donlan, R., & Whitaker, T. (2019). *The school board member's guidebook.* New York, NY: Routledge.

Eadie, D. (2003). *Eight keys to an extraordinary board-superintendent partnership.* New York, NY: Rowman & Littlefield Education.

Elmore, R. (2004) *School reform from the inside out.* Cambridge, MA.: Harvard University Press.

Elmore, R. (2007). Professional networks and school improvement. *School Administrator, 64* (4), 20–24.

Friedman, Thomas L. (2016). *Thank you for being late: An optimist's guide to thriving in the age of accelerations.* New York, NY: Farrar, Straus, and Giroux.

Fullan, M. (2011, April). *Choosing the wrong drivers for whole system reform.* Seminar series 204. Melbourne: Center for Strategic Education.

Fullan, M. (2011). *The moral imperative realized.* Thousand Oaks, CA: Corwin.

Fullan, M. (2019). *Nuance: Why some leaders succeed and others fail.* Thousand Oaks, CA: Corwin.

Fullan, M., & Edwards, M. (2017). *The power of unstoppable momentum: Key drivers to revolutionize your district.* Bloomington, IN: Solution Tree.

Fullan, M. , & Quinn, J. (2016). *Coherence: The right drivers in action for schools, districts, and systems.* Thousand Oaks, CA: Corwin.

Fullan, M., Quinn, J., & Adam, E. (2017). *The taking action guide to building coherence in schools, districts, and systems.* Thousand Oaks, CA: Corwin.

Fullan, M., Quinn, J., & McEachen, J. (2018). *Deep learning: Engage the world change the world.* Thousand Oaks, CA: Corwin.

Gemberling, K. W., Smith, Carl W., & Villani, J.S. (2000). *The key works of school boards guidebook.* Alexandria, VA: National School Boards Association.

Goodman, T. (2014). *The battle for the customer is interface.* Oath Tech Network. Retrieved from https://techcrunch.com/2015/03/03/in-the-age-of-disintermediation-the-battle-is-all-for-the-customer-interface

Gottlieb, H. (2001). *Why boards micro-manage and how to get them to stop*. Help 4 NonProfits. Retrieved from http://help4nonprofits.com/ NP_Bd_MicroManage_Art.htm

The Group of Thirty. (2012). *Toward effective governance of financial institutions*. Washington, DC: Author.

Hammond, L.D. (2010). *The flat world of education*. New York, NY: Teachers College Press, Columbia University.

Hanberg, E. (2015). *The little book of boards: A board member's handbook for small (and very small) nonprofits*. Tacoma, WA: Side x Side Publishing.

Hargreaves, A., & Fullan, M. (2012). *Professional capital transforming teaching in every school*. New York, NY: Teachers College Press, Columbia University.

Harvey, T., & Drolet, B. (1994). *Building teams, building people*. Lancaster, PA: Technomic Publishing Co.

Heifetz, R., & Linsky, M. (2002). *Leadership on the line: Staying alive through the dangers of leading*. Cambridge, MA: Harvard Business School Press.

Houston, P., & Eadie, D. (2002) *The board-savvy superintendent*. Lanham, MD: Scarecrow Press, Rowman & Littlefield.

Howell, W. G. (Ed.) (2005). *Besieged school boards and the future of education*. Washington, DC: Brookings Institution Press.

Kurzweil, R., & Meyer, C. (2003). *Understanding the accelerating rate of change*. Kurzweil Accelerating Intelligence Essays. Retrieved from http:// www.kurzweilai.net/understanding-the-accelerating-rate-of-change

Lencioni, P. (2011). *The Five Dysfunctions of a Team*. San Francisco, CA: Jossey-Bass.

Long Beach Unified School District Board of Trustees. (2003). *Governance handbook*. Long Beach, CA: Long Beach Unified School District.

Malkin, E., & Paulina, V. (2018, October 20). Faced with reality of job, Mexico's next president scales back promises. *New York Times*. Retrieved from https://www.wral.com/faced-with-reality-of-job-mexico-s-next-president-scales-back-promises/17933849/

McAdams, D. R. (2005). *What school boards can do: Reform governance for urban schools*. New York, NY: Teachers College Press, Columbia University.

McCain, John. (2009). Remarks by Senator John McCain at the memorial service for Senator Ted Kennedy. Retrieved from https://www.mccain .senate.gov/public/index.cfm/speeches?ID=70fa80b8-e62c-423e-dac4-1af9740eb68a

Merriam-Webster. (2018). Uniform. Retrieved from https://www.merriam-webster.com/dictionary/uniform

Mulder, P. (2012). Communication model by Albert Mehrabian. *ToolsHero.* Retrieved 2018 from https://www.toolshero.com/communication-skills/ communication-model-mehrabian/

Nicoll, J. W. (1995). *So you want to be a superintendent?* Sacramento, CA: School Services of California.

North Monterey County Unified School District. (2018). *Governance Handbook.* Retrieved from https://www.nmcusd.org/cms/lib/CA02204777/ Centricity/Domain/49/Governance%20handbook%202018.pdf

Payne, C. M. (2008). *So much reform, so little change: The persistence of failure in urban schools.* Cambridge, MA: Harvard Education Press.

Quinn, J., McEachen, J., Fullan, M., Gardner, M., & Drummy, M. (2019). *Dive into deep learning: Tools for engagement.* Thousand Oaks, CA: Corwin.

Rosenberger, M. K. (1997). *Team leadership school boards at work.* Lancaster, PA: Technomic Publishing.

Schein, E. (1999). *Process consultation revisited: Building the helping relationship.* Reading, MA: Addison-Wesley.

Senge, P., Kleiner, A., Roberts, C., Ross, R., & Smith B. (1994). *The fifth discipline fieldbook: Strategies and tools for building a learning organization.* New York, NY: Doubleday Publishing.

Senge, P., Kleiner, A., Roberts C., Ross, R, & Smith B. (1999) *The dance of change: The challenge of sustaining momentum in learning organizations.* New York, NY: Doubleday Publishing.

Smith, C. J. (2000). *Trusteeship in community colleges: A guide for effective governance.* Washington, DC: Association of Community College Trustees.

Sonnenfeld, J. (2002, September). What makes great boards great. *Harvard Business Review.* Retrieved from https://hbr.org/2002/09/what-makes -great-boards-great

Thompson, C. (2015). Building collaborative leadership skills: A primer, part II. Retrieved from http://www.thefundneo.org/our-blog/building-collaborative-leadership-skills-primer

Tuttle, E. M. (1958). *School board leadership in America: Policy making in public education.* Danville, Il: The Interstate Printers and Publishers.

Vollmer, J. (2010). *Schools cannot do it alone: Building public support for America's public schools.* New York, NY: Enlightenment Press.

Waters, J. T., & Marzano, R. J. (2006, September). School district leadership that works: The effect of superintendent leadership on student achievement: A working paper. Mid-continent Research for Education and Learning (McREL). Retrieved from https://www.ctc.ca.gov/docs/default-source/educator-prep/asc/4005rr_superintendent_leadership.pdf

Williams, P. (with Ford, T.). (2010). *Bear Bryant on leadership: Six lessons from a six-time national championship coach.* Charleston, SC: Advantage Media Group.

Yankelovich, D. (2001). *The magic of dialogue: Transforming conflict into cooperation.* New York, NY: Simon & Schuster.

Index

Acknowledgments

This book is the product of over thirty years of working with governance. We have seen it all. The great, the good, the meh, and the very ugly. Through it all, we have remained deeply committed to the importance of strong, quality governance in education. As a result, we are optimistic. The reason for our optimism is that we have personally witnessed the dedication, skill, and commitment of trustees and superintendents working together to provide quality education for all children. The Governance Core described in our book is the result of these experiences. We have a great deal to be thankful for from countless individuals and organizations. We thank them all. Some that deserve special recognition are listed below.

From Davis: None of this would have been possible without the partnership developed over the past years with the gifted governance leaders, trainers, and facilitators in the California School Boards Association (CSBA). For me, personally, three stand out: Leslie DeMurrsiman, former President of CSBA, the incredible fighter for quality and a dedicated trainer; Sherry Loofbourrow, also former President of CSBA, the calm, studious deep governance thinker, and Babs Kavanaugh, perhaps the best facilitator and governance/policy trainer I have worked with. The fingerprints of all three are all over this book. It is difficult to mention everyone who had an impact on this work. Virtually all leadership of CSBA over the years contributed to building these ideas. But special recognition needs to go to the late Maureen DiMarco, long-term school board trustee and President of CSBA, the first Secretary of Education and Child Development in California, a friend and colleague and one of the best governance thinkers ever. I also want to acknowledge those dedicated, courageous, and committed school board trustees and superintendents who have led the way to effective governance in some of the most difficult times we have experienced. Special acknowledgement needs to be given to Paul Richman, former Chief of Staff of CSBA and former Executive Director of the California Parent Teachers Association (PTA). Paul, a great writer, provided both insight and editorial comments at a time when both were needed. Going back to the beginning, a special thank you to the brilliant community leader and lifelong advocate for excellence in education, Marion Joseph, who by her force of will, got me started on this professional journey.

And of course, my personal partner for 49 years who has been an inspiration and supporter, my wife Jan, without whom nothing would have been possible.

From Michael: I have learned about governance from many fabulous superintendents and directors (as we call them in Ontario) over the years. In all cases, the most effective ones developed strong bonded partnerships with their boards. Thanks to Bill Hogarth, John Malloy, Denise Andre, Laura Schwalm, Chris Steinhauser, and Sandy Thorstenson for the opportunities to learn from them—lessons upon lessons as they adapted to the challenges of evolving governance. My team, too numerous to mention here, has become a cadre of great "system leaders" around the world in the districts, municipalities, states, and provinces in which we work. I learn from them every day. My family—wife Wendy and sons Bailey and Conor—serve to some extent as my personal board. Thanks for avoiding micromanagement while ensuring that the fundamentals are always in order.

From both of us: Our publisher, Corwin, knows a thing or two about governance. A dream publisher providing great guidance and stimulation, Corwin has a combination of superb individuals and even better teams, thereby modeling what we write about in this book. Thank you to our direct Corwin team: Arnis Burvikovs, Desirée Bartlett, Eliza Erickson, Melanie Birdsall, Lynne Curry, and many others behind the scene.

About the Authors

Davis Campbell is the former Executive Director of the California School Boards Association and is Chair of the University of California, Davis, School of Education, Board of Advisors and a Senior Fellow. He also serves as a Trustee on the Stuart Foundation Board of Trustees.

Campbell has a deep and broad background in public education. He served for 12 years in the California Department of Education, serving six of those years as Deputy State Superintendent of Public Instruction in charge of all education programs. In 1988, he was appointed Executive Director of the California School Boards Association, serving in that capacity until his retirement in 2001. He also served as an elected trustee on the Yolo County Board of Education.

Campbell maintains an active consulting practice in effective governance in education as well as public and nonprofit agencies at both the state and international level. In California, in addition to trainings and workshops with school districts, most recently he conducted workshops in governance for new and first-time superintendents. He has conducted numerous workshops with nonprofit organizations as well as training sessions with cities, counties, and special districts. Campbell's international governance work includes board support for the American School of Madrid (15 years), the American School of Barcelona, the American School of Paris, the American Cooperative School, Tunis, Tunisia, the American International School of Egypt, and effective governance workshops in Lisbon, Portugal, and Rome and Milan, Italy.

Michael Fullan, OC, is the former Dean of the Ontario Institute for Studies in Education, and Professor Emeritus of the University of Toronto. He is co-leader of the New Pedagogies for Deep Learning global initiative (npdl. global). Recognized as a worldwide authority on educational reform, he advises policymakers and local leaders in helping to achieve the moral purpose of all children's learning. Michael Fullan received the Order of Canada in December 2012. He holds honorary doctorates from several universities around the world.

Fullan is a prolific, award-winning author whose books have been published in many languages. His book, *Leading in a Culture of Change*, received the 2002 Book of the Year Award by Learning Forward, *Breakthrough* (with Peter Hill and Carmel Crévola) won the 2006 Book of the Year Award from the American Association of Colleges for Teacher Education (AACTE), and *Turnaround Leadership in Higher Education* (with Geoff Scott) won the Bellwether Book Award in 2009. *Change Wars* (with Andy Hargreaves) was named the 2009 Book of the Year by Learning Forward, and *Professional Capital* (with Andy Hargreaves) won the AACTE 2013 Book of the Year, and the Grawemeyer Award in Education in 2015.

Michael Fullan's latest books are *The Principal: Three Keys for Maximizing Impact; Coherence: Putting the Right Drivers in Action* (with Joanne Quinn); *Deep Learning: Engage the World Change the World* (with Joanne Quinn and Joanne McEachen); *Surreal Change: The Real Life of Transforming Public Education* (autobiography); and *Nuance: Why Some Leaders Succeed and Others Fail.*

For more information on books, articles and videos, please go to www .michaelfullan.ca.

A SAGE Publishing Company

Helping educators make the greatest impact

CORWIN HAS ONE MISSION: to enhance education through intentional professional learning.

We build long-term relationships with our authors, educators, clients, and associations who partner with us to develop and continuously improve the best evidence-based practices that establish and support lifelong learning.

INTERNATIONAL

Leadership That Makes an Impact

LYN SHARRATT

Explore 14 essential parameters to guide system and school leaders toward building powerful collaborative learning cultures.

MICHAEL FULLAN

How do you break the cycle of surface-level change to tackle complex challenges? *Nuance* is the answer.

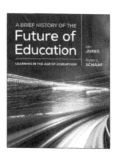

IAN JUKES & RYAN L. SCHAAF

The digital environment has radically changed how students need to learn. Get ready to be challenged to accommodate today's learners.

ERIC SHENINGER

Lead for efficacy in these disruptive times! Cultivating school culture focused on the achievement of students while anticipating change is imperative.

JOANNE MCEACHEN & MATTHEW KANE

Getting at the heart of what matters for students is key to deeper learning that connects with their lives.

LEE G. BOLMAN & TERRENCE E. DEAL

Sometimes all it takes to solve a problem is to reframe it by listening to wise advice from a trusted mentor.

PETER M. DEWITT

This go-to guide is written for coaches, leaders looking to be coached, and leaders interested in coaching burgeoning leaders.

ANTHONY KIM & ALEXIS GONZALES-BLACK

Designed to foster flexibility and continuous innovation, this resource expands cutting-edge management and organizational techniques to empower schools with the agility and responsiveness vital to their new environment.

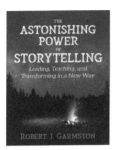